BASIC ILLUSTRATED

Alpine Ski Touring

BASIC ILLUSTRATED

Alpine Ski Touring

Molly Absolon

WITHDRAWN

FALCON GUIDES

GUILFORD, CONNECTICUT
HELENA, MONTANA

FALCONGUIDES®

An imprint of Rowman & Littlefield
Falcon and FalconGuides are registered trademarks and Make Adventure Your Story is a
trademark of Rowman & Littlefield.

Distributed by NATIONAL BOOK NETWORK

Copyright © 2016 by Rowman & Littlefield

All interior photographs by Molly Absolon, unless otherwise noted

British Library Cataloguing-in-Publication Information available

Library of Congress Cataloging in Publication Data available

ISBN 978-1-4930-1847-5 (paperback)
ISBN 978-1-4930-1848-2 (e-book)

♾™ The paper used in this publication meets the minimum requirements of American National
Standard for Information Sciences—Permanence of Paper for Printed Library Materials, ANSI/NISO
Z39.48-1992.

Contents

Snow transforms the natural world into a magical place. ALLEN O'BANNON

Introduction

The first time I went backcountry skiing was in the late 1980s. I was on skinny telemark skis, wearing leather telemark boots that barely rose above my ankle. I managed to link a few wobbly turns, and a 20-degree slope felt plenty steep, which meant the experience wasn't really about the skiing—it was about the place.

I'd never been out in the winter before. Never experienced the stillness of a forest coated in sparkling snow or the thrill of painting a blank slope of untracked powder with my tracks (ugly as they were in those days). I'd never seen the telltale signs of a weasel hunting in a snow-covered meadow or followed the path of a porcupine dragging its belly through the powder.

Even the stormy side of winter thrilled me. The sound of the wind, the challenge of keeping warm, the intensity of making real life-and-death decisions about where to go, what to ski, and how to communicate all gave the adventure a power that hooked me.

Today's lightweight, high-performing alpine touring gear has opened up the backcountry to skiers. Lynne Wolfe

As the years passed, the old telemark gear morphed into today's modern alpine touring gear, and with that my attraction to backcountry skiing shifted. Now the allure is not just the magic of winter in the mountains, it's also the thrill of skiing powder and skiing it well—on bomber alpine touring equipment, with the heel locked down, rather than doing telemark turns on the

More and more people are stepping outside the boundaries of ski resorts to enjoy the backcountry.

gear of yore (although there are some who still enjoy that unique challenge). I'm not alone in making this transition. Today's alpine touring gear is light and high performing. Long gone are the wobbly turns of old. Now you can ski steep, technical terrain on gear that is also comfortable for a long uphill "skin" (ascending using climbing skins on your skis).

This shift in equipment has resulted in a boom in the backcountry ski industry. Alpine touring (commonly referred to as AT) is the fastest-growing segment of the snow sports industry. No more are the days when you were guaranteed fresh shots of untracked snow if you were willing to hike. Now some of the best stashes get tracked out quickly. But even with that, there's so much incredible backcountry to explore that it's usually possible to get away from the more crowded areas and find solitude.

This growth in alpine ski touring has some unintended consequences. It's really easy now for people to get in over their heads quickly. In places like the Wasatch Range outside Salt Lake City, Utah, you can be backcountry skiing after less than an hour of hiking from the trailhead. Even easier, it's possible to simply step outside resort boundaries into what some people call the sidecountry: the unpatrolled, uncontrolled terrain reached through exit gates along the edges of resorts throughout the world. Such ready access coupled

Backcountry skiing entails taking responsibility for your own safety. There is no avalanche control or ski patrol once you leave a resort's boundaries. JOHN FITZGERALD

with the addictive pull of powder is attracting larger numbers of skiers and snowboarders into the backcountry—some of whom have no business leaving the resort area.

When people get in over their heads, it's usually not the skiing that challenges them. That part is easy, especially with today's equipment. What gets

Understanding snow takes years of experience and study. When you first head into the backcountry, go with someone who can help you learn. JOHN FITZGERALD

people in trouble is their understanding of the hazards of backcountry travel and the responsibility they assume for their own safety when they leave a resort. You are on your own out there—there's no ski patrol and help can be hours away—and the potential hazards you face are many. Avalanches are undoubtedly the direst danger, but you may also encounter challenging weather, injuries or broken equipment that can quickly change a half-day romp in the mountains into a deadly epic.

This book is intended to help the beginner backcountry skier understand what alpine touring entails. We'll talk about equipment, technique, route selection, and hazards. Reading about these things will help you educate yourself so you know the questions to ask and the guidance you need to venture out of bounds safely. But you can't just rely on a book. If you plan to pursue alpine touring, find a mentor. Take an avalanche class. Pick a modest objective while you gain experience. Ignorance can be deadly. Start slowly so you don't become a statistic.

CHAPTER 1

Alpine Touring Equipment

Alpine touring gear is hot, hot, hot. It's where some of the most creative innovation is occurring in the ski industry. Every year skiers are given more options for boots, skis, bindings, and other essentials.

Alpine touring is the fastest-growing snow sport for good reason. Skiing untracked powder is fun!

As with any new sport, choosing the right equipment can be overwhelming. Do you want a super-stiff boot or a soft one? How long and wide should your skis be? What features are critical in a backcountry ski pack? You can find lots of this information online or from a reputable ski shop, but it is nice to have some basic knowledge to filter your search, which is where this book can help you.

Bindings

Bindings are the distinguishing feature that defines alpine touring. If you have ever tried to walk very far in your downhill ski gear, you'll know that it's almost

Alpine touring bindings allow you to free your heel for ascending and then lock it down for descending.

impossible. AT bindings take care of that problem by allowing you to free your heel so that you can walk or climb comfortably on your skis, and then lock your heel down for the descent. It's this ability that makes it possible for you to tour and turn in your ski equipment.

Before the advent of the AT binding, most people used a telemark binding to access the backcountry. Your heel is always free in a telemark binding, making touring easy. Telemarking is still popular with some skiers, but the telemark turn definitely requires more skill to master than an alpine turn, and so telemark gear never revolutionized backcountry skiing the way the AT binding has.

The first AT bindings, also called randonee bindings, were made for alpine climbing. They were designed to be used with mountaineering boots to access a peak, and for that purpose they worked well, but they did not release in a fall. As people began to push into the backcountry to make turns rather than reach summits, those bindings no longer fit the bill. Lots of innovation occurred over the subsequent years, but it was really the Italian company Dynafit that revolutionized the sport when it came out with a lightweight binding that performed well both on the approach and on the descent. For years Dynafit had a patent that protected its binding design, and so its products were pretty much the only option if you wanted to go light. But a few years ago, that patent ended, and now there are a number of companies making lightweight AT bindings.

Two Types of AT Bindings

There are two basic categories of AT bindings: frame and tech. Frame bindings have toe and heel pieces that are connected by rails or a frame so that the entire piece moves up and down when you free your heel. These bindings often work with both downhill and alpine touring boots, which is an advantage if you already own ski boots and don't want to buy a new pair for alpine touring.

Tech bindings traditionally rely on a set of pins that attach the toe and heel of your boot to the binding, although there are some models now that have different modes of attachment for the heel. For these bindings, you need a special AT ski boot.

Deciding which style of binding is for you depends on the following factors:

- What kind of skiing do you plan to do? (Touring, mix of resort and backcountry, aggressive free skiing, etc.)
- What type of skier are you? (Level, style, fitness, size, etc.)

- Are you willing and able to carry the extra weight of heavy binding in exchange for higher performance on the descent? Or are you willing to accept limitations on the descent for a lighter binding?

In simple terms, frame bindings are going to be best for heavy, aggressive skiers who spend most of their time in steep, demanding terrain close to the resort or accessed by a helicopter. These bindings release more reliably than a technical binding in the event of a fall. They are also heavier, allowing them to push through crud or hold an edge on hardpack with very little deflection. The downside is they add pounds to your feet, and that takes a toll on a long day in the backcountry. Plus, they can feel clunky and awkward on the skin track.

Tech bindings are lighter on the uptrack, but they don't have quite the same performance or release capabilities of a downhill binding. So in some

Setting the Release on Tech Bindings

Many tech bindings do not meet the International Organization for Standardization requirements for alpine ski bindings (ISO 9462).

Unlike an alpine binding that releases laterally at the toe, tech bindings release both laterally and vertically at the heel. In general, tech bindings are less predictable in a fall than a downhill binding. For people who fall a lot, that may be enough of a difference to cause you to choose a frame AT binding. But bindings are improving every year, and there are models (the Dynafit Beast and the Marker Kingpin to name two) that come close to having the same release capabilities as a downhill binding.

To figure out the appropriate settings for your tech bindings based on your size, weight, and skiing ability, you can use an online calculator. But the best bet for beginners is to go to the ski shop or consult a knowledgeable, tech-savvy friend.

The rationale for the settings on a tech binding is somewhat cryptic—you won't just use the same DIN setting you use on your downhill skis. You need to consider both vertical and lateral forces, which gets confusing. So initially have a ski mechanic adjust your binding, but ask him or her to show you how to make changes. That way if you find you are releasing at inopportune moments, you can change the setting on your own.

A ski tech can also make sure that the spacing behind your heel is correct.

situations—say on steep, firm snow or if skiers are heavy or aggressive—you may notice a difference. But these bindings—often called Dynafit bindings after the original manufacturer—are what revolutionized backcountry skiing. They make touring for turns enjoyable, and, in most cases, will be the binding of choice for alpine tourers because of their light weight and versatility.

Using Your Tech Bindings

Tech bindings are a bit harder to use than your normal downhill binding. You don't just step in and go. So it behooves you to practice with your setup standing on the carpet in your living room rather than find yourself futzing around in the wind and cold at the top of a run.

To click into your AT binding, line up the holes in your boot with the pins on the binding's toepiece and step down. To ensure your boot is locked in properly, swing your foot back and forth. The movement should be even and smooth.

To start, press the lever at the front of your binding down to open the wings and spread the toe pins apart. If you are touring first, turn your heelpiece so that the pins are off to the side. If you are skiing down first, the pins on the heelpiece should face forward toward your heel.

Line the holes on either side of the toe of your boot with the pins in the binding's toepiece and step down. Modern bindings have bumpers to help

When touring, raise the toe lever to lock the ski on. You can do this by placing your pole under the lever and pulling up.

you place your foot in the correct spot, and many boots come with some kind of mark to help you line the holes up. If your boots don't have a mark, take a black Sharpie pen and make your own. It can be tricky to line up your boots properly, so practice.

If you have difficulty getting into your binding or the binding is releasing for no reason, you probably have snow or ice in the holes of your boot preventing the pins from setting properly. Ice can also build up in the space below the binding wings under the toe. Some people carry a nail in their pocket to help clear those spots. That can be especially helpful if you are skiing in wet conditions where ice buildup is more common.

Once your toe is locked in place, gently swing your foot back and forth a few times to make sure it is secure. You shouldn't feel any wobbliness. If you do, check for ice buildup.

Now place the ski flat on the ground, hook your ski pole under the tab of the binding directly in front of your toe, and pull up to lock the toes in place for touring. (If you are about to descend, leave the toes unlocked.)

If you are touring, you are good to go.

AT bindings have some kind of heel lift that allows you to lessen the angle between the sole of your boot and the slope, which makes ascending steeper slopes more comfortable. ALLEN O'BANNON

For ascending, AT bindings will have some way to raise your heel to allow you to walk more comfortably up a slope. To access your heel lifts, you may have to rotate the heelpiece or you may have to flip up some kind of platform for your heel to rest on. Take time to practice raising and lowering your heel lifters using just your ski pole. You don't want to have to stop and bend over on the ski track to make this maneuver.

When it's time to descend, turn the heelpiece so the pins are facing your boot and stomp down. If your toes are locked, it's wise to push the lever down to unlock them. Unlocking the toepiece is safer as you are more likely to eject in the event of a fall with the lever down. There are rare occasions when losing a ski can be deadly, so you may opt to keep your toes locked in these extreme situations.

Skis

Theoretically any ski can be used as a backcountry ski. It's really the binding that determines the difference. But as alpine touring has gained popularity, more and more ski companies are designing skis specifically for it. What this mainly means is that the skis are lighter, which is important when you plan to take thousands of steps dragging them along underfoot as you move through the mountains.

To determine the right ski for you, you need to define who you are. Just as with choosing a binding, the right ski depends on things like your skiing

Backcountry skis come in all shapes, widths, and weights. This display of skis is from a shop in the Rockies where most buyers are looking for fat powder skis.

ability, your fitness and body type, your ski goals, and the terrain and snow-pack you are most likely to encounter on your tours. Do you ski in Sierra cement or Wasatch blower pow? Are you dropping into firm couloirs or seeking out hidden stashes in the trees? Do you mainly ski corn, powder, or "frozen granular"? The answers to these questions will determine what kind of ski you should be looking for.

Remember, in the backcountry you don't have the luxury of traversing to a groomer if the snow conditions get gnarly. You have to get down the mountain regardless of whether it's covered with breakable crust, wind slab, or frozen chunder, even if that means traversing the slope and making a kick turn to change directions. The impact of this on your choice of ski is simply that you need to look for skis that are versatile and can handle a variety of conditions, especially if you can only afford one pair.

Width

In simple terms, the firmer the snow conditions you expect to encounter, the narrower the ski you will want to ride. If most of your adventures take place on long spring tours where you won't have deep powder or if you are a rando racer who wants to move fast on the uphill, you'll want a ski with a waist between 70 and 90 mm. These skis are lighter for the ascents and nimble and quick on the descents, but they don't perform as well as fatter skis in fresh snow or variable conditions.

If you expect to be skiing powder or variable snow, you'll want to go wider, probably with a ski that is between 90 and 115 mm at the waist. These skis are usually a bit heavier but will offer more stability in variable conditions and more float in the powder.

Shape and Profile

Backcountry skis generally sport either a traditional profile with some camber underfoot or a hybrid one that includes an early rise or rocker tip, some tapering at the waist, and a flat tail. Narrow skis usually sport a traditional profile to provide the most contact with the snow and, therefore, more edge hold for turning in firm, hard-packed snow.

A hybrid ski profile comes into play as the ski gets wider. An early-rise tip helps the ski float through powder and bust through crud. The camber underfoot provides contact with the snow on climbs and edge contact for turning on the downhills.

Fully rockered skis or skis with wonky shapes and funny tips and tails are less common in the backcountry than at the resort, mainly because they don't hold skins very well. You need a ski with tip and tail that you can attach your climbing skins to securely, and you also need one that flattens out when

---

Camber vs. Rocker

Camber is an arced space that forms between the tip and tail of a ski when you lay it on the ground. When you weight a cambered ski, that arc flattens out and the entire ski comes into contact with the snow. Camber puts springiness and pop into your ski and creates a powerful carving tool, especially on hard-packed snow.

Rocker is a reverse camber. When you place a fully rockered ski on the ground, the central part of the ski will make contact while the tip and tail are uplifted. Rockered skis help keep your tips up out of the snow, and because there is less edge contact with a rockered ski, it's easy to initiate a turn with them. The downside to rocker is that the skis feel squirrely on hard-packed snow because you have less edge contact. Many modern skis include a combination of rocker and camber to maximize the benefits of both.

weighted to allow it to come into contact with the snow so you have enough grip to move up the skin track without slipping backward.

Length

Alpine touring doesn't really affect your length choice in skis. You'll ski the same length on your backcountry skis that you ski on your alpine skis. If you are new to the sport, get an expert's advice. In general, people ski narrow skis longer than wide ones.

Materials

The biggest difference between a resort-specific ski and a backcountry ski is the weight, which is determined by the materials used in construction. Backcountry skis are lighter than resort skis so you have to move less weight as you tour. The weight savings come from using lighter materials in the core— carbon fiber, bamboo, beech, and poplar are some examples of the types of materials used to shave off ounces.

The lighter the ski, the more chattery it tends to be on hardpack. Heavy skis can dampen the unevenness of the snow surface, but a light ski gets knocked around. It can be somewhat disconcerting to look down at your tips when cruising down a groomer at a resort on a pair of lightweight backcountry skis and see them bouncing around. But in soft snow you won't notice a difference, and the weight savings means your legs will be less fatigued.

Picking a Model and Brand

Ski manufacturers make skis for just about everything. There are bump skis, park skis, powder skis, racing skis, women's skis, trick skis—you name it, you can find it. Narrowing down your selection can be challenging.

Every year, ski magazines such as *Backcountry* do a review of the new models. This can be a place to start your search, as the testers will comment on all aspects of a given ski's performance in various conditions. Ski stores are another place to get information, although it helps to come with some knowledge to ensure the salesperson steers you in the right direction. Online forums offer gear reviews that can help you wade through the flood of options available. Just remember as you do your research that a ski that is appropriate for a 250-pound man may not work for a 125-pound woman and vice versa. Look at who's doing the reviewing before you follow his or her lead.

If you can, test out some different models to see what you like. These days ski shops will rent out an entire backcountry setup, including safety equipment, so you have an opportunity to try things out before you lay down the big bucks and make a purchase.

Ski swaps and consignment stores can be a great place to pick up a screaming deal on a pair of used skis, and, if you are just starting out, that may be a good place to start. It's easy to drop $1,000 on new skis, but if you are a beginner or someone who just gets out a few times a season, that kind of expenditure is unnecessary. Be realistic about your goals and honest about your abilities when you go shopping.

Caring for Your Skis

To maximize your skis' performance, you need to keep them tuned. First and foremost, skis should be waxed relatively often so they glide freely and are easier to turn. Wax makes the skis hydrophobic—resistant to, or "afraid of," water—and prevents suction from developing between your ski base and the snow, which can slow you down. Many people wax their skis daily, others don't. You know it's time when the base appears chalky or your friends out-glide you on the out-track. Waxes are designed for specific temperature ranges. In general, wax warm if you are uncertain. Cold wax will feel slow. You can find how-to videos online that walk you through the process of waxing your skis. Here's just one example: www.youtube.com/watch?v=bXJMw4gLmGM.

If you get divots or core shots in your base from hitting rocks, fill the holes with ptex to keep the base smooth and fast. You can do this at home—again instructions are easy to come by online—or take your skis into a shop for a tune-up.

Skiing in icy, hard conditions will dull your edges. Carefully run your finger down your ski edge, and if you feel burrs or rough spots, your edges need sharpening. If you are predominately skiing powder, edges are less critical to performance, but your skis will last longer if they are well maintained.

Ski Poles

If you plan to do a lot of backcountry touring, it's worth investing in a pair of telescoping poles that allow you to adjust the length so you can make them longer for touring and shorter for descending. Look for ski poles with a big basket. The little ones you see in resorts don't work well in soft powder. Non-adjusting poles are fine if you don't want to fork out the money for adjustable poles, but they are definitely less versatile. To test for the appropriate length, stand the pole upright on the ground, handle down, and grip it with your hand below the basket. Your elbow should make a 90-degree angle. You can fudge that angle a little bit and go for a slightly longer pole to help with touring if you opt not to go for adjustable poles.

You can buy poles that also act as probes in the event of an avalanche. However, most backcountry skiers carry a separate probe rather than rely on their ski poles. Ski pole probes can be hard to put together quickly and are often not long enough.

Boots

Like skis, more and more ski boot manufacturers have begun to offer back-country ski touring boots as part of their lineup, so these days you have a lot more choices than you had even a couple of years ago. Also like skis, your boot choice will largely be dictated by your goals, ability, size, and shape. AT boots are not cheap. It's hard to find a model that sells for less than $500 and all too easy to find one costing more than $1,000.

AT boots feature a lugged rocker sole like a hiking boot that allows for easier walking and has some grip on slippery surfaces. They also include a walk mode that unlocks the ankle cuff so you flex your foot back and forth as you walk.

Stiffness

The stiffer the boot, the more responsive it will be to your subtle body changes as you make turns. That means skiers who seek out steep terrain where quick jump turns and precise edge control are essential are going to want a stiff boot. But for powder skiing, that stiffness is less critical, and you can get away with a softer, more comfortable boot. Be honest with yourself. Do you really need a super-stiff boot for the kind of skiing you'll be doing? It's great to have a high-performing boot, but if you are a low-performing skier, that's overkill and you may find yourself hating life when you are midway up a 2,000-foot climb.

There are lots of different AT boots on the market these days. To help choose the right boot, think about your goals. If you plan to spend a lot of time touring in the backcountry, don't underestimate the importance of comfort.

Some boots also come with a tongue that can be removed for touring and replaced to add stiffness for the descent. These kinds of features mean even a stiff boot can be relatively comfortable on the ascent if it fits properly.

Angle

Historically, high-performance ski boots featured an aggressive forward angle. That is changing as modern, carving skis have come into play. You no longer need to be pitched way forward to move your skis around and stay out of the backseat. Newer boots feature a more neutral, upright stance that is easier on the quads and more centered and balanced over the skis.

Weight

AT boots range in weight. Often the most expensive boots are the lightest. The weight savings come from the use of carbon fiber and thinner shells. Weight does make a difference, especially on long approaches, but shaving a few ounces is less important than finding a boot that fits well.

Ski-mo boots—or AT boots designed for ski mountaineering—are superlight, but they aren't made with turns in mind. Rather, these highly

> **Boot-Fitting Tip**
>
> It's not uncommon for you to experience cramping in new boots or on your first couple of tours of the season. There's a good chance this is caused by tension rather than boot fit, especially if a good boot fitter checked yours out. Lots of people unconsciously curl their toes or try to initiate their turns with their feet, causing them to cramp. Your feet may also just be rebelling at being clamped into a tight boot after a summer in flip-flops. Try to relax your toes and loosen your buckles to see if that helps. Most likely the cramping will stop after your first day out.

specialized boots are designed for climbing. Unless you plan to get into ski-mountaineering racing, you will not want these boots.

Comfort

Comfort is the number-one consideration in an AT boot in the opinion of many backcountry skiers. On a long tour you don't have the luxury of going into the lodge to take off your boots and ease your aching feet. You need a boot you can hike in for hours that also performs well when it's time to descend.

To ensure you have a comfortable boot, go to a reputable store and have someone fit you. You take a big risk buying a boot online without trying it on. You don't want a boot that pinches your feet or cuts off your circulation, making your feet cold and causing blisters, but you also don't want something that feels sloppy.

AT boots usually come with a moldable thermal liner made from insulating foam. These liners can be heated up for a customized fit, helping improve comfort and performance.

Climbing Skins

Climbing skins are strips of napped fabric that you apply to the bottom of your skis to provide traction for ascending. Historically, climbing skins were made from sealskin, hence the name. Today most are made from nylon, mohair, or a nylon/mohair blend. The nap in the fabric points back toward the tail of your ski, so it lies flat as you slide forward but backward motion causes it to stand up. Think of running your hands through the fur of a dog: In one direction the dog's coat is smooth, but rub it the other way and it stands on end. These upright fibers provide traction as you move uphill in your skins.

Most skins come with tip and tail attachments, although there are people who prefer not to use tail clips. These attachments help secure the skin to your ski, but the real stick comes from an adhesive or glue on the back of the skin that adheres to the base of your ski.

Materials

The materials used for your climbing skins will affect their performance. Nylon is known for its grip and durability, but it tends to have less glide than mohair. Mohair, made from the hair of angora goats, glides best but wears faster and can be less grippy on the uphills than nylon. Mohair/nylon blends offer characteristics of both materials and end up falling in the middle in terms of performance.

These differences are subtle. For inexperienced skinners, there may be no appreciable difference. In fact, if you are a beginner, nylon skins may be the best option because they are easier to climb in. Ascending an uptrack takes skill. A good skinner can climb a steep, icy track that will send a beginner slipping back down the hill. We'll talk about technique later in the book, but for now know that if you are just starting out, you probably don't need to worry too much about the material used for your skins.

Width

Skins perform best when they cover the entire base of your skis with just the metal edges sticking out (there can be some exposed areas around the tip or tail without sacrificing performance). To determine the correct width for your skis, measure them at their widest point and subtract 5 to 6 mm.

Most skins require trimming. You may be able to buy a model that is designed specifically for your ski, in which case all you need to do is pull the skins out of the package and you are good to go. Other brands have to be cut for length and trimmed along the edges to get the best coverage. Trimming is easy, but it takes time and patience so don't leave it for the morning of a tour. Skins come with a trimming tool and directions. If you take your time and follow the directions, you'll have no trouble customizing your skins to your skis. (See evo.com/how-to-trim-cut-ski-climbing-skins.aspx for guidelines.)

Glue

Manufacturers have experimented with glueless ways to secure skins, but for now, the most reliable skins are glue-ons. The trick to maintaining your glue's performance is to keep it clean and free of dirt, dog hair, pine needles, and other materials that diminish its adhesive capacity.

Different skin manufacturers use different glues. Check with dealers or read reviews on the glue used on any brand you are considering. Some glues don't perform well in extreme cold or wet snow, so it is helpful to know that before you make your purchase, especially if you know most of your skiing will be taking place in a cold or wet place.

You'll preserve your skins best if you take care of them. It doesn't take much, but a few critical habits will ensure the skins last years instead of months.

When you finish your ski tour, your skins will probably be wet. Hang them up to dry at home. Glues are sensitive to heat, so don't leave your skins in the direct sun on the dashboard of your car or any place where the heat can be intense. Just let them dry at room temperature. Also don't store them for the summer in a hot attic. A cool or even cold room is the best place to store skins in the off-season.

Skins come with a cheat sheet or strip of plastic webbing that adheres to the base of your skin, making them easier to pull apart. You can store your skins with the cheat sheet in place if you want, but for most use you'll want to discard it and just fold the skins together, glue-side in, between uses. The cheat sheet just adds an unnecessary step in your transition process. The only exception to this is with brand-new, super-sticky glue that takes shoulder-popping strength to pull apart. In this case, it is worth using the cheat sheet until the glue gets a little lest sticky.

Glueless skins come and go on the market. In general, they have yet to perform well enough to surpass traditional glue-on skins. But it's worth keeping an eye on them as manufacturers work on improvements. Currently glueless skins fall short in terms of their ability to retain sticking power. Often they will work well for one lap uphill, but if you plan to make multiple ascents, the skins lose their stick.

Skin Wax

In wet conditions it is common for snow and ice to build up on the bottom of your skin. This buildup quickly multiplies until you find yourself with several extra pounds of snow stuck underfoot. The best way to avoid the snow and ice buildup is to anticipate its potential before you head out. Snow sticks when your skins get wet. So if it's wet out, you'll want to prepare. There are rub- and spray-on waxes that can be applied to a dry, warm climbing skin to repel water and keep the skin from icing up. They don't work very well if your skin is already wet, so plan ahead and apply the wax before you head out.

Applying and Removing Skins

The first step to putting your skin onto your ski is to make sure the base of the ski is snow free. Then pull an arm's length or so of the skin apart so the glue

To put your skin on, place the holder over your tip, hook the ski into your hip, and pull toward you. Attach your tail clip and smooth the skin onto the base of your ski.

is exposed, and place the tip hanger over the tip of your ski. Press that top section of skin into place, making sure it is centered so the metal edges are exposed. Push the tip of your ski away from you and pull apart the rest of the skin. Hook your tail clip on and make sure the skin is centered, then smooth it down with your hand and you are ready to go.

Some skis come with special skins that attach differently (such as Dynafit skis). If you have this kind of setup, ask the dealer how they recommend you take your skins on and off.

You can remove your skins without taking off your skis, but it takes some balance and practice. The simplest method of removing skins is to simply click out of your binding, pick the ski up, unhook the skin's tail clip, and strip the skin off halfway. Grab the midpoint of the freed section of skin and fold it in half, glue side to glue side. You will now have half of your skin neatly folded. Next, pull the remaining half of the skin off the base of your ski, grab the middle with one hand, and fold the skin in on itself, and your skin is ready to stash in your pack.

If you want to try to remove the skin without taking off your ski, make sure you are in a flat area and are well balanced. Lock your heel down into ski mode, then lift the tail of your ski up so that you can reach behind to unhook

To remove your skin without taking off your ski, lock your heel down, then lift the tail of the ski so you can detach the tail clip. Pull the skin forward and away, lifting your tip to help you get the right angle to separate the skin glue from your ski base.

the tail clip. Pull the skin down and away from you, lifting your tip in the process. With sticky glue, this can be hard, but once you master the technique, it's fast and you'll move through your transition from climbing to skiing quickly.

Ski Backpacks

There are countless backpacks on the market, and whatever you have in your closet can work for a ski pack. But if you really plan to get into alpine touring, it's worth investing in a pack specifically designed for ski touring. Why? Because these packs are made with the vagaries of winter in mind. Remember, it's cold out there in the winter, and the last thing you want to do is dig around your backpack for 5 minutes to find an essential item. It's nice to have a pack that allows you to manipulate the zippers and open toggles without having to take off your gloves, and having your avalanche rescue gear easily accessible is critical.

Size

For backcountry skiing, look for a pack with roughly a 30-liter capacity. That gives you enough room to carry extra layers, repair equipment, food, water, and your avy gear. You may be able to get away with a smaller pack, but you don't want to be tempted to leave essential safety gear behind because of space issues. Plus it's a pain to struggle to fit everything into a tight space with your gloves on, so roomier is better.

Features

Most AT skiers like to have a separate storage compartment for their avalanche shovel and probe. That way you can leave your gear stored in your pack all the time. Make sure these compartments are easily accessible and secure. When you need your avalanche rescue gear in an emergency, you don't want to have to unpack everything to find it or to discover your probe fell out because a Velcro flap came undone.

Check to see how the pack is designed to carry skis. Different brands have different methods—A-frame or diagonal are the most common styles out there—and you want to make sure the pack you choose has an easy attachment system that you can manipulate with your gloves on.

It's nice to have easy access into your backpack in the winter when gloves limit your dexterity.

A lot of AT skiers like to be able to get into the main body of the pack without having to go in through the top. Some backpacks feature a zippered-clamshell opening on the underside that gives you access to your stuff. Others come with a side zipper that lets you into the guts quickly. Not everyone likes this feature and an extra zipper does add weight, but if you want that kind of convenience, it's worth looking for. Otherwise, you probably don't want a lot of external bells and whistles on your ski pack. Extra ice ax loops, attachment points, and zippered pockets all add weight. If you don't think you'll use a special feature, don't go for a pack that includes it.

Many packs feature an internal water-bladder pocket and a place for a hose in the shoulder strap. This can be nice and will help you stay hydrated during the day. The key thing is to ensure the hose is insulated and the bladder is stored close to your back in the pack so the water doesn't freeze. You can also start the day with warm water in the bladder to reduce the chance of it freezing.

Avalungs

On average it takes 20 minutes to find and dig out an avalanche victim. Survival rates for those buried more than 15 minutes drop off rapidly, with most deaths from asphyxiation occurring between 15 and 35 minutes. Black Diamond Equipment makes an Avalung pack with a hose and mouthpiece that you bite down on if you get caught in an avalanche. Breathing through an Avalung extends the time you can be buried beneath the snow up to four times as long as you could last without it.

The Avalung works by pulling in fresh air from the surrounding

The Avalung pack has a breathing tube and mouthpiece that allows you to breathe oxygen out of the surrounding snow. Make sure you have the mouthpiece unzipped and in a ready position before dropping in. (Some people even ski sketchy slopes with it already in their mouth.) John Burbidge

snowpack, creating an artificial air pocket from which you can get oxygen. When you exhale into the tube, the Avalung pushes the CO2 away from the area of intake. There is very little hard data on the effectiveness of the Avalung because it hasn't been tested in real-life situations often, but in a few cases it has saved someone's life. Obviously you don't want to get buried in an avalanche, but an Avalung can be a valuable tool for enhancing your survivability if that should happen, so it's worth considering carrying one.

Airbags

More and more companies are making backpacks that include an inflatable airbag. The idea is that a skier can inflate the bag if he or she is caught in an avalanche. Airbags work on the principle of inverse segregation: Items with the greatest volume naturally rise to the top when they get shaken up. You've seen this before. Think of popcorn: When you finish your bowl, all the unpopped kernels are left on the bottom after the fluffy popped stuff floats to the top. Likewise, if you are in an avalanche, an airbag will add volume to your mass and help keep you on the surface. Staying on the surface is important. The Swiss Federal Institute for Snow and Avalanche Research has found that 53 percent of people who are buried in an avalanche die, while only 4 percent of those who are caught but stay on top do. So airbags can help keep people alive.

Airbags have their limitations. They do not protect you against trauma, so if a slide takes you through trees or over a cliff, they may not help. In small slides the airbag may not have time to get you to the surface, or if there is a terrain trap, the snow may pile up so deeply you get buried anyway.

Airbags are also not always used correctly. In all too many avalanche accidents, the victim

Airbags are designed to keep you on top of an avalanche if you get caught. Victims are more likely to die if they are buried in debris. John Fitzgerald

wore an airbag but did not deploy it. Airbags are also expensive, heavy, and complicated. It takes practice to learn to use one, and you can't always carry your airbag on an airplane because of its detonating device. That said, the technology continues to improve, and more and more avalanche experts are advocating their use. It's worth researching airbag backpacks as you pull together your AT touring kit. If you are an expert skier, it's likely you'll end up on slopes that have the potential to slide. An airbag gives you a backup plan if you blow the call in terms of assessing a slope's stability and end up caught in an avalanche.

Pack Fit

Like all backpacks, you want to make sure your ski pack fits well, or you'll be uncomfortable on a long tour. To check the fit of a pack, loosen all the straps before putting it on your back. Load some weight into the pack so you get a sense of what it will feel like when you go out for a tour. Now put it on your back.

Once the pack is in place, snug the hip belt down tightly. You'll want it to rest on top of your hipbones—on the iliac crest—snugly. That's where most of the weight of your pack should ride. Make sure that you have at least an inch of clearance on either side of the belt buckle to allow for adjustments as you add or subtract clothes. Now tighten the shoulder straps. They should wrap closely around your body to pull the pack forward, but they should not be holding the weight—that stays on your hips. The attachment points for the shoulder straps should fall about 1 or 2 inches below the top of your shoulder.

If your pack has load-lifter straps running from the top of the shoulder strap to the backpack, cinch these down now. This strap should make a 45-degree angle between your shoulder and the pack. The load-lifter straps help pull the weight of your pack off your shoulders, but not all ski packs have them.

Now slide the sternum strap up or down on your shoulder straps to the appropriate height—approximately nipple level—and buckle the strap across your chest to pull the shoulder straps in away from your armpits. If the pack has stabilizer straps on the hip belt, cinch these down to pull the pack in closer to your hips. Finally, loosen the shoulder straps slightly.

If the pack is the appropriate size, you should feel most of the weight on your hips. The pack should ride close to your back so that it won't pull you off balance when you are making turns, and you should feel very little weight in your shoulders.

Safety Equipment

Unless you know you are traveling in terrain that is incapable of producing an avalanche, all AT tourers should carry basic avalanche safety gear. We'll go into more detail about avalanche terrain later, but in general, slopes over 30 degrees are suspect in most parts of the United States. To give you an idea of what that looks like, an expert slope at a ski resort is usually around 30 degrees or steeper, so if you ski black terrain at the resort, it's likely you'll ski avalanche terrain in the backcountry.

Basic avalanche safety equipment includes an avalanche transceiver (also called a beacon), a probe, and a shovel. There are many manufacturers making this equipment, and we won't go into endorsing any particular brand. The key is to know your gear and understand how to use it so that in an emergency you aren't bumbling around trying to figure it out while your buddy is buried.

Choose a probe that is at least 2 meters long and assembles quickly and easily. Look for one with measurements marked on the side. The markings help in a snow pit when you are analyzing conditions and can also tell you how deep someone is buried. If your probe isn't marked, use a permanent Sharpie pen to make your own measurement markings.

Your shovel should be collapsible and made from aluminum. The blade should be at least 3,000 cubic centimeters.

Beacons

Every avalanche transceiver, or beacon, is tested to ensure it meets specific performance criteria before it is released to the market. So if you buy a reputable brand, you'll be fine as long as you know how to use it. You want to be able to search effectively and quickly in an emergency, which takes practice. So play around with finding buried transceivers before you have to.

Also, beacons must be turned on to work. There are lots of stories of people who come home from a day's tour and realize they never turned their transceiver on. Check the battery at home before leaving. Make a habit of switching on your beacon the minute you put it on your body. Turn it off when you get home at the end of the day. As you start touring from your car, check your partners to make sure their beacons are transmitting.

> **Handheld Radios**
>
> Most ski guides carry handheld radios to communicate with their clients, and more and more recreational skiers are following suit. Radios are useful when skiers are separated and want to talk to one another, which happens frequently when you ski avalanche slopes one person at a time or when skiing in the trees where it is hard to keep tabs on one another.

What to Carry on a Day Tour

Winter travel means being prepared for anything. Temperatures are often bitter cold or uncomfortably warm if the sun comes out and the snow is acting like a reflector oven. The wind can bite, and precipitation can soak. You need to be prepared to take care of yourself if weather conditions change, your equipment breaks, you get injured, or, worst-case scenario, someone gets caught in an avalanche. So even on a day tour, you should carry a number of basic essentials to ensure you can hunker down and survive if you end up stranded.

Clothing

The basic attire for a backcountry skier starts with a base layer on the top and bottom made from either wool or some kind of synthetic fabric like Capilene. These long-underwear layers are like your second skin and usually don't come off until you are back in the warmth of your home. On top of your base layer, you'll add and subtract clothing throughout the day according to temperature.

On the bottom you'll usually just need some kind of ski pants over your long underwear. These can be softshell water-resistant pants, or if it's wet or snowy, you may opt for waterproof shelled pants. Look for ski pants with a built-in gaiter to secure over your boot and keep the snow out. Zippers down the side for ventilation are also nice. Insulated ski pants used in the resort are almost always too hot for touring.

On top, start with a base layer and a windproof jacket with a hood. This jacket can be a water-resistant softshell, or, for stormy weather, you'll be better off in a waterproof shell. Look for ventilating zippers under the armpits and a hood that can be cinched down so it stays in place and doesn't block your vision. If it's really cold, you may want to wear a second insulating layer on your torso—say an expedition-weight zip-T, a pile sweater, or a down vest—otherwise your base layer will usually suffice.

The key to staying comfortable in the winter is layering your clothing so you can add and subtract items as the conditions change.

On your feet wear wool or synthetic socks, and on your hands opt for some kind of water-resistant glove or mitten that comes up over your wrist. A wool or pile hat for your head tops off your basic touring outfit.

Inside your pack you'll want more layers so you can add and subtract clothes as the conditions change and your activity level varies. An insulated

> ## Basic Day-Tour Clothing List
>
> - Wool or synthetic base layer: top and bottom
> - Wind and water-resistant shell: hooded jacket and pants (Consider waterproof shells for stormy, wet weather.)
> - Optional midweight top layer (extra expedition-weight top or lightly insulated jacket for cold days)
> - Insulated jacket with hood (consider insulated pants in cold temperatures)
> - Two pairs of gloves or mittens (one lightweight pair for ascent, insulated pair for descent)
> - Two hats (one lightweight, one medium weight)
> - Neck gaiter

jacket made from down or some kind of synthetic material is great to throw on when you stop to rest. Hooded jackets are most versatile because pulling up the hood greatly increases the coat's warmth. If the temperatures are really cold, it is a good idea to also include a pair of insulated pants in your daypack. Make sure you can zip the pants on without having to remove your boots.

Bring along a spare pair of insulated gloves or mittens. Often your hands will get wet on the ascent, and it's nice to be able to change into something warm and dry for the ski down. Gauntlet gloves that come above your wrist are helpful for keeping the snow out, and a sticky or leather palm is nice for gripping your ski poles.

Finally, a neck gaiter or balaclava is key for adding insulation and protection for your face as conditions change. A lightweight nylon neck gaiter can double as a headband that keeps hair and sweat out of your eyes on warm days. And if you get sweaty feet, it's smart to throw a spare pair of socks into your backpack for emergencies.

Sunglasses and Goggles

Your basic touring kit should include sunglasses and ski goggles. Even when clouds hide the sun, its glare is hard on your eyes and can cause painful snow blindness, so sunglasses are essential. But they usually don't provide enough protection for skiing down in a snowstorm, so it's important to carry goggles in your pack as well unless you know the weather will be clear. Goggles typically fog up quickly if you wear them on the uptrack or push them back on

You'll need sunglasses or goggles to protect your eyes even on overcast days. ANDREW MORLEY

top of your head. Your best bet is to tuck them into your backpack when not in use.

Helmet

More and more skiers are wearing helmets, even in the backcountry. It's worth thinking about carrying one, especially if you are skiing in trees or rocky areas. They don't weigh much and can save your life.

Avalanche Rescue Equipment

As mentioned before, you should always carry a shovel, transceiver, and probe with you on all day tours. Your transceiver should be worn on your body one layer out from your skin (not carried in your pack). The other items can be stored in a convenient spot in your pack for quick access in an emergency.

Food and Water

Carry plenty of food and roughly two liters of water on all day tours. You may choose to bring an insulated bottle for tea, hot chocolate, or soup. Your water bottle or bladder should be insulated so it doesn't freeze during the day.

Personal Items

Make sure you have sunscreen, lip balm, and a headlamp in your pack. A scraper for getting ice off the bottom of your skis and a nail for poking it out of your bindings are useful tools to keep handy in a pocket.

Repair Kit (Day Touring)

A small repair kit is essential, although not everyone in your party needs to carry his or her own. Just make sure that your group has the following:

- multi-tool
- spare binding parts (screws, spacers, etc.)
- zip ties for linking together broken binding parts
- spare basket for ski pole
- duct tape (can be wound around a ski pole or water bottle)
- extra ski straps (include some that are long enough to wrap around your boot in case a buckle breaks)
- gob-stopper wax if you are headed out in the spring when the snow is wet
- parachute cord, because it is always handy

First Aid

As with your repair kit, not everyone in the group needs to carry a first-aid kit, but make sure your group has athletic tape, blister-care supplies, pain-relief medication such as Ibuprofen, latex gloves, a compact mask for rescue breathing, and basic wound-care supplies. Chemical hand and foot warmers are also useful to have stashed in your pack for an emergency.

Emergency Bivouac Gear

Not every backcountry skier carries emergency "bivy" gear along on day tours, but it is something to consider, especially if you plan to be far from your car. At a minimum a lighter and candle or some kind of fire starter are useful items to stash in your pack just in case you get stranded in a forested area and want to build a fire to help keep you warm.

You can also carry a waterproof bivy bag or a space blanket and a small piece of closed-cell foam or Ensolite to help you stay off the ground and reasonably warm in the event of an unexpected night out.

CHAPTER 2

AT Technique

This book is not about downhill skiing technique. Presumably you are already a skier and are reading this to allow you to step outside the resort boundaries and enter the backcountry.

If you are not a skier, it's worth spending some time at a ski area perfecting your downhill technique before you venture out. Take some lessons, watch other people, and practice on slopes with lift access before you start hiking. You'll get a lot more turns in that way and will improve much faster than you will in the backcountry, where you tend to spend more time hiking up than skiing down.

This book will focus on the part of backcountry skiing that is different than resort skiing, namely *touring*.

Skinning

The Skinning Motion

The basic movement for touring on skis is the kick-and-glide. It's a natural movement—you're just walking in your skis—but it helps to break things down so you understand how to be more efficient. On lightweight cross-country skis, the kick-and-glide lets you move along at a rapid pace. On AT skis you'll usually have skins on and your skis tend to be fat and clunky, so don't expect to do much more than walk or shuffle.

To start, put your boots in walk mode and loosen the buckles so you can flex your ankle back and forth as you move.

Now slide one foot forward. Use your hip flexor and glute to drive your knee uphill. On an existing skin track, you'll want to keep the bottom of your ski in contact with the snow to maximize your traction. If you are breaking trail, you may need to punch down through your heel to lift your tip up out of the snow.

Flex your forward ankle so your knee is bent directly above or slightly ahead of your toe. Shift your weight onto that leg, pushing off with your back foot. Stand upright on your forward leg and draw your back leg forward, keeping the ski sliding on the surface of the snow. Plant the moving foot

Skinning is really just walking across the snow on your skis, but it's important to center your weight over your feet to keep you from sliding backward. ALLEN O'BANNON

ahead of your standing foot—how far ahead depends on the terrain. On a hill your stride will be short; on the flats it will be longer. Now shift your weight onto the new forward foot, and push back with your opposite leg to move yourself forward. Repeat over and over again until you reach your destination.

Let your arms swing along naturally, planting your pole beside your foot with each stride. The pole plant and push gives you some added impulsion, but you don't want to rely on your arms to move you uphill. Your legs and butt should do all the work. If your arms are tired or your shoulders are sore at the end of the day, you are pushing on your poles too hard.

Your stride should be as long as possible on the flats to allow you to ride out any glide you get from your kick. You'll save energy this way. When you encounter an uphill, shorten and quicken your stride to maintain traction. Don't lift your feet with each step. Instead drive your knee forward, sliding your ski along the snow. Your goal is to keep as much contact between your ski and the snow as possible. Make sure to keep your body upright. If you lean too far forward, you won't weight your skis underfoot and the fibers of your climbing skins will have less purchase on the snow, causing you to slip backward. Ultimately, even with climbing skins, you will reach a steepness where the grip of the skin is not sufficient for the angle of the slope. At this point

If you lean too far forward as you ascend, you don't weight your skis as effectively as you do when your weight is centered and upright, causing you to slip. Try to stand as upright as possible. ALLEN O'BANNON

you'll need to either cut a lower-angle switchback or move into other uphill techniques to continue to ascend.

Beginners have a tendency to shoot their forward leg too far ahead, so their knee is behind their extended foot and their toes are pointed. The problem with this is that you cannot weight the forward foot efficiently. Try to keep your body weight forward, with a slight bend at the waist and your shoulders just ahead of your hips. That will allow you to keep your weight centered over your skis and ensures the most traction from your skins.

Heel Lifters

Heel lifters—also called heel elevators or risers—ease the stretch in your Achilles tendons and hamstrings as you skin uphill. Raising the heel creates an angle between the bottom of your foot and the top of your ski that allows you to minimize the forward flex of your ankle as you move upward. Some people go quickly to their heel lifters, others do not. It depends on your ankle flexibility, the angle of the skin track, and your skinning expertise.

Most AT skiers tour with skins, which minimize their gliding potential. If you have a long flat approach, consider using kick wax on your skis. Some people may cringe at the idea of contaminating the base of their ski with anything but glide wax, but when you have 2 miles to shuffle up a snowmobile road before you even begin to climb, skins will feel painfully slow and cumbersome. With wax, you may actually feel the flow of the kick-and-glide technique as you move over rolling terrain.

Uphill-Climbing Techniques

In places the slope may become too steep for you to ascend using your kick-and-glide technique, or you may not have skins on and you need to climb out of a drainage or up a short slope and it isn't worth stopping to skin up. In these situations, you can use either a herringbone or side-step technique.

Herringbone

The herringbone is quick and effective but gets tiring fast so it is best suited for very short sections of uphill. To perform a herringbone, spread the tips of your skis apart and bring your tails together to form a V-shape with the V opening uphill. Roll your ankles inward slightly so the inside edges of your skis bite into the snow. Step one foot forward and up and weight that ski. Bring your downhill foot up beside and slightly ahead of the uphill one, shift your weight onto that ski, and then move your first foot up again. Continue moving from foot to foot until you reach the top of the slope.

Make your pole plants fall slightly behind your body. This helps keep your weight back. If you lean too far forward, your skis will slip backward. The more upright you stay, the more your weight will push down on the edges of your skis and the better grip you will maintain.

Use the herringbone technique to ascend short sections of uphill without putting on your skins.

Side Step

The side step is exactly what it sounds like. You turn your skis perpendicular to the slope's fall line—or the line a ball would follow if it were to roll downhill—and climb sideways up the hill. You'll need to roll your ankles slightly uphill to set the uphill edge of your ski, which gives you the traction you need to ascend. Most people find that moving slightly forward and up with each step is less strenuous than simply ascending vertically.

Side stepping can be challenging in AT gear because the tail of your skis flops down, making it hard to move it up evenly. If you anticipate a long section of side stepping, it is probably worth locking down your heels to save energy and increase efficiency. If you don't want to stop to lock down your heel, keep your foot close to the snow as you move it up, leading with your tip and dragging the ski up. This requires smaller steps but will help you move the ski up more effectively.

Skinning Downhill

You don't really choose to skin downhill, but inevitably you will encounter places where you need to descend while wearing skins during the course of your approach. If the downhill section is short, it's usually not worth taking off your skins, but beware: Descending on skins with your heels unlocked is unnerving. You'll feel unbalanced and the skins don't glide evenly or predictably, so even the best downhill skiers get pitched around at times. Lower your heel lifts if they are up. Point your skis across the fall line if possible to reduce the angle of the slope. Try to keep your weight back on your heels so you don't end up doing a face plant if your skis slow unexpectedly. Consider locking your heels for added stability. Don't attempt to make turns, just look for a nice, straight line that you can coast down, coming to a stop naturally at the bottom. Often you'll find descending in skins easier if you move off the packed trail and into fresh snow, which will naturally slow you down.

Skinning Turns

We'll talk more about setting an uptrack later in this chapter, but for now know that on almost all ascents, you are going to have to change direction along the way. Most climbs are too steep to go straight up so the uptracks tend to zigzag uphill in a series of switchbacks, all of which require a turn at each end.

Walking Turns

On gentle terrain, the easiest way to change direction is to simply walk around the turn. Some people call this the A-V turn because your skis

I've Fallen and I Can't Get Up!

Inevitably you will fall. Usually it's when you are skiing down, but people do tip over on the skin track and, more commonly, when they encounter a downhill section with their skins on and heels free. When you fall, consider dumping your pack to make it easier to get up, especially in deep snow. Then untangle yourself so you end up with your skis perpendicular to the fall line and below you. This may require some maneuvering. Don't be afraid to use your hands to help move your skis around.

Once you're in position, take your poles and make an X with them on the surface of the snow uphill of your body. This is especially important in deep, soft powder that won't support your weight. Place your uphill hand in the center of the X, and use it as a platform to push down on. You can also use your backpack as a platform if you chose to remove it.

Push yourself forward onto one knee and then stand up. Brush off the snow and you're off again.

It helps to have a platform to push off of when you are trying to get up after falling in soft snow. Make an X with your poles and press down on the center or use your pack to provide some support as you rise.

alternate between an A-shape with the tips together and a V-shape with the tails together.

To perform a walking turn, try the following:

1. As you step forward with your downhill ski, angle the tip out slightly so your skis form a V-shape with the tails together. Be sure to keep the bottom of your ski in contact with the snow, which may require you to roll your ankle slightly to the inside.

2. Now drag your outside ski forward, rotating the ski tip toward the downhill ski so you end up with your tips together, tails apart, just opposite of the angle you were in for the first move. This will be your A. Again, make sure that ski maintains contact with the snow by rolling your ankles or adjusting the length of your stride.

3. Keep repeating this process until you've walked a gentle arc around the corner and are facing the opposite direction from where you began.

The most energy-efficient way to change directions going uphill is to simply walk around the corner. Start with your skis in a V-shape, then bring the tips together into an A, and then step back to a V and repeat until you have reversed directions.

Kick Turn

As the slope steepens, walking turns become challenging, so you may need to switch to a kick turn to change direction. We'll start with the basic uphill kick turn and then explain a downhill variation that you can use if you run into a tight spot, obstacle, or snow conditions where you can't turn uphill.

Setup

As you set your uptrack, think about where you will need to make a change of direction and ease back on the angle of the track as you approach that point. On steep terrain or slippery snow, aim to have your skis perpendicular to the fall line with your tails at the same level as your tips before you start your turn. In lower-angle terrain or fresh powder, you can do your kick turn on a bit of a slope. Stomp down on your skis to get a good solid stance, especially if the snow is hard.

The Turn

a. From your platform, shift all your weight onto your downhill ski, planting your downhill pole beside your hip for balance. Place your uphill pole above you and off to the side, high enough so that your ski can clear it as it swings by.

b. Lift your uphill ski, letting the tail drop down behind the heel of your downhill boot. Keeping the tip of your ski high, arc it around like a windshield wiper until the tip is facing the opposite direction from the tip of your downhill ski. Your tail will come up and around as you make this move.

You will now be in fifth position if you ever took ballet—feet parallel with your heel next to the toe of the opposite foot. (It's worth practicing this move on flat terrain because it can be challenging and requires some flexibility!) Make sure you keep your skis across the fall line or you may find yourself slipping and falling in a very awkward position. Move your downhill pole up beside your uphill pole for balance.

c. Transfer your weight to the uphill ski and lift the downhill ski up off the snow. If you have springs in your bindings, you can just swing the

---

Tip: Drive the Tail into the Snow

If you find you have trouble getting your ski around, try shoving the tail of your uphill ski into the snow underneath your downhill ski right beneath the heel of your downhill boot. You can make this easier by punching a hole in the snow next to your boot with your ski pole to drive your ski tail into. This trick helps if you have trouble with hip mobility in the turn.

(A) *Establish a stable platform to begin your kick turn. As the slope gets steeper, your platform will need to be more perpendicular to the fall line to ensure you don't slip backward while negotiating the turn.* **(B)** *Lift your inside ski and slide it back, arcing the tip away from you toward your new direction of travel.* **(C)** *Drive the tail of your inside ski underneath the ski you are standing on. If the snow is too hard, punch a hole with your pole for the ski tail. This step helps keep you from doing the splits as you try to step around your turn and is also useful for those with less flexibility.* **(D)** *Weight your inside ski, lift the other ski, and swing the tip around so the skis are parallel and facing your new direction of travel.* **(E)** *Off you go!*

downhill ski around until it is parallel to your other ski and facing in the same direction. If your tail dangles down, give it a little punch through your heel as you rotate your hip and leg inward to bring the ski around. That will pop the tip up and drop the tail, allowing you to rotate the ski. You should now be facing the other direction and ready to continue on your merry way.

Downhill Variation

There are times—on steep terrain or if there's an obstacle in your way—when you cannot turn uphill. In such cases, a downhill kick turn is a good alternative.

a. You'll set up in the same way you did for the uphill turn, making sure you have a good, stable platform. But for a downhill turn, you are going to be moving downhill as you negotiate the turn, so stomp out your platform and then move slightly above it before you start the turn. Plant both poles downhill for stability and balance.

b. Set the edge of your uphill ski. Slide the downhill ski forward, then rotate your foot around so the ski arcs 180 degrees and ends up facing the opposite direction from the uphill ski.

c. Once the ski is facing the opposite direction, step down onto it. Your feet will be in ballet's fifth position: the heel of the downhill foot below the toes of the uphill foot and vice versa. Make sure you are stable and then shift your weight onto the downhill ski.

d. When your weight is on the downhill ski, raise the tip of your uphill ski and slide the ski forward along the side of your downhill boot, then rotate the ski around 180 degrees until the tip is downhill and parallel to the ski you are standing on. If the tail drops and keeps you from getting the ski all the way around, kick through the heel to pop the ski around. Step onto your downhill ski and continue off in the opposite direction.

Tip: Spotting a Kick Turn

If you can get in a good, solid position, you can spot your partner on a kick turn, which can be helpful if the snow is firm and turning feels tenuous. Stand below the person negotiating the turn and use your poles to support the edge of the downhill ski while she moves her uphill ski around.

Ski Crampons, Ice Ax, or Whippet

On early spring mornings before the sun softens the snow or on north-facing slopes in the alpine zone, you may find yourself confronting icy, firm surfaces where skins do not provide enough traction to allow you to ascend. For these conditions you may feel more secure and confident with ski crampons. Not everyone likes ski crampons and there are some outspoken critics of their

In steep, icy conditions it's nice to carry a tool like this whippet ski pole that allows you to stop yourself in case you take a fall.

use, but for long gentle climbs on icy snow, they can make life much more enjoyable.

As mentioned earlier, ski crampons fit under your boot and wrap around your ski so that their metal teeth bite into the snow when you step down. Most technical bindings have a groove right behind the toepiece where the crampon slides in.

Once the crampon is in place, click into your binding like normal and start walking. Walk with your feet slightly farther apart than normal to ensure the crampons don't catch on each other. Drag your skis up the track and step down firmly, punching down through your foot with a little extra pressure to set the teeth firmly in the snow. Don't lift your foot and stomp: As with skinning, you want to maintain contact with the snow at all times to maximize your traction. You may find you need to roll your ankles a little to keep your skis level on the snow.

Sometimes it's easier to climb a bit steeper with crampons than you would without, but beware: The crampons can give you a false sense of security, letting you venture out onto slopes that are steeper than is appropriate without an ice ax or some other form of protection to stop you in the event of a fall. If you lose control and slip on such a slope, you may go for a long,

In the spring the snow is often hard and icy during your ascent. Crampons can be invaluable in such conditions.

dangerous ride. This is the reason some people don't like ski crampons. So pay attention to the surrounding terrain as you move upward and don't waltz out onto an exposed icy slope without evaluating your route. Remember, it's difficult to reverse course once you've committed yourself.

In really steep, icy terrain, you should carry an ice ax, use boot crampons, and climb the slope with your skis strapped on to your pack. Some manufactures make a ski pole with an ax included on the handle, or you may be able to find an ice ax attachment for your poles. Or just carry an ice ax. The ax allows you to create a secure attachment point to the slope as you move upward. The big thing to remember in these conditions is that if you fall, it will be very hard to stop or self-arrest. The snow is just too hard. You need to feel confident in your ability to use your ice ax as a self-belay as you ascend. These are no-fall conditions. If you don't feel comfortable, use a rope, protection, and a belay. All these techniques require instruction in their proper application, so make sure you seek it out before putting yourself in a dangerous situation.

Setting a Track

As you venture out into the backcountry, you will run into all kinds of uptracks. Some people like to set steep lines that go straight up the slope;

The best uptracks follow natural lines of weakness and are never so steep that you are fighting to keep from slipping backward with every step.

others zigzag back and forth with low-angle switchbacks. You may find yourself making kick turn after kick turn or following a long traversing line with very few turns. None of these tracks are right or wrong. What matters is that the track is functional, efficient, and safe. Setting an uptrack is an art that takes vision, experience, and skill.

Angle

The type of uptrack you set will be determined by a number of different factors, including the terrain, your group's skill level, and the snow conditions.

We'll get into avalanche terrain later in the book, but your number-one consideration when establishing a skin track is picking a safe line. You move slowly when skinning uphill and therefore are vulnerable to avalanche

When establishing an uptrack, choose a line that avoids avalanche terrain, such as ridges, low-angle slopes, or heavy timber.

hazards for a long time if your track runs across a dangerous slope. So it's key to choose a line that stays in safe terrain. Look for ridges, low-angle slopes, heavy timber, and other signs that the area is free from avalanches to set your track and watch out for what's above you. You may be in a flat meadow, but if there's an avalanche path looming overhead, you are in danger.

It behooves you to consult a contour map before you head out, especially if you will be traveling in unfamiliar terrain. The map can help you identify potential hazards, pick out a good route, and locate landmarks that will keep you oriented throughout the day.

Generally speaking, low-angle tracks are more energy efficient and hold up better with use than steep ones. On a steep track you need to shorten your stride and exert more effort to step up; as a result, you tend to take more steps to cover the same amount of ground as you would on a low-angle track where you can lengthen your stride. A lower-angle track also allows you to pace yourself and conserve energy. You'll move more steadily on a low-angle track, and it's easier to keep your heart rate consistent so you don't flame out too early in the day—but don't go too flat or you'll never reach your destination. There's a happy medium, and you'll just have to experiment some to figure out the best angle for you and for your objective.

Some people recommend setting a skin track that has an average 14 percent grade, others would set that number higher. It's hard to know what a 14 percent grade looks like, so better gauges for setting the angle of your skin track are:

a. You can maintain a conversation as you hike.

b. There aren't places where people are slipping or falling or struggling to move upward.

Planning Your Line

Before you head up the hill, step back and look at the terrain. Pick out a rough path for ascending the entire slope, not just the little section right in front of you. Look for good places for turns and traverses. If you can, plan to walk around your turns rather than making a kick turn at each end of your switchback. Kick turns take more energy than a simple walking turn.

Choose a contouring line that winds its way up around land features without gaining unnecessary elevation. Give yourself plenty of space to maneuver when it's time to change direction. Evaluate the uptracks of others. Figure out what works and what doesn't. You can even have someone more experienced follow behind you and coach you on where to make turns and how steeply to climb.

Efficiency

You spend most of your time AT touring on the skin track. It's not uncommon to climb for 4 or 5 hours for a descent that takes 30 minutes, so it is important to pace yourself. Most people find ascending at a rate of roughly 1,000 feet an hour is a good, moderate pace that they can maintain over the course of a long day, so aim for that goal as you set out.

It's also a good idea to stop at regular intervals—say every hour for 5 minutes—to have a drink and eat a snack. You'll be using a lot of calories exercising and moderating your body temperature in cold weather, so eat a lot and drink frequently to maintain your energy level throughout the day.

Pacing is important if you plan to be out for a long day in the mountains during the winter. Stop to refuel and rest at regular intervals so you don't flame out early in your adventure.

Snow Conditions

Powder

Deep snow is great for descending but less great for climbing. It takes energy to break through fresh powder, especially if it is heavy, but the effort is well worth the reward.

Breaking trail in fresh powder is hard work. Take turns out front to conserve your energy for the downhill.

Breaking trail through powder is best done as a team effort where you cycle through leaders to conserve energy. When you are out front, you will be working hard, but once you fall behind your teammates, the going gets easy. So take turns leading. In really difficult conditions you may shift places every 5 minutes; when the going is easier, you can take longer stints out front. But remember to save your energy for the downhill, and don't break all the trail when there are others behind you who can take a turn.

One of the biggest challenges in deep snow occurs when your tips dive down deep beneath the surface. Pulling them up and out of the snow takes

---

Work-Hardening Snow

Uptracks generally improve after a few passes because the snow "work-hardens," or bonds together, to form a strong, cohesive unit that supports you on the surface of the snow. Think of a snowball: You pick up a handful of powder, roll and pat it between your hands, and voilà! In the right conditions you have a perfectly formed ball that holds together. That's work-hardening.

---

a lot of effort. Use the highest setting on your heel lifters for breaking trail in deep snow as they help keep your tips up. As you move forward, flip your tip up and out of the snow by punching down through your heel with each step. That will help keep your ski at an angle above the snow and the tip on the surface—or at least not deeply buried. Sometimes you may need to pull your ski back toward you to clear the tip.

Sugar Snow

Faceted or sugary snow is difficult to set a track in because the crystals don't bond together or set up as you work-harden them, and you may find yourself floundering around and sliding backward as the snow around you collapses. Faceted snow is common after extended cold, dry snaps, on north-facing slopes, or around trees. Your best bet if you run into faceted snow is to try to find better snow—so head to a different aspect where the sun makes the snow more cohesive. Sometimes, though, you just have to fight your way through the sugary snow. Keep the angle of your uptrack low and take time to stomp out your foot placement before you commit your weight to it. Don't get frustrated. Usually you can find a way to easier terrain.

Boot Packing

It's common to find boot-pack routes in the side-country next to a resort or at heavily used areas like Mount Glory off Teton Pass in Wyoming. Here you see a lot of skiers who just carry their alpine skis and hike in their downhill boots rather than invest in an AT setup, which means they need to boot rather than skin uphill. Also, boot tracks are important in places where you don't have room to traverse, like up couloirs in the high peaks.

Boot tracks are common in couloirs where you don't have space to set a traversing skin track.
John Fitzgerald

Breaking Trail

Unlike a traversing switchback, the best boot-pack tracks go straight up with no turns or traverses. Your line will be dictated by the terrain. Ideally you can find a route up a ridge that keeps you out of avalanche terrain, but if you are in a couloir, that will not be an option. You'll need to evaluate the snowpack before you commit to the climb, because once you are in the couloir, you are in direct line of fire from snow slides coming down from above.

You need to be very confident in the snow's stability before you begin booting up a couloir, because you are in the line of fire of anything coming down from above as you climb.
JOHN FITZGERALD

> ## Rest Step
>
> The rest step is a mountaineering technique designed to conserve energy during a long, steady climb. To perform the rest step, weight your uphill foot and move your downhill leg up, straightening the weighted leg completely as you move so your bones rather than muscle tension support your weight. Don't hyperextend your leg: Just make it straight enough for your skeleton to hold your weight. Pause in this position for a moment and then repeat on the other side. The best rest-steppers time their breathing to their steps, moving at a slow, even pace that they can maintain for hours. Try it. It's a great way to moderate your pace so you can keep going and going and going. . . .

To set the track, lift your knee with your hip flexor until your boot is clear of the snow, swing your foot forward, hinging at the knee and letting the weight of your boot provide momentum as it comes into contact with the snow. You don't need to create a huge step with lots of kicks unless the snow is hard (in which case crampons may be the weapon of choice). Ideally you just need a kick or two to establish a platform large enough to hold your weight—usually that will be no more than 3 inches deep. Step up keeping your weight straight over your foot. If you lean too far forward, you are likely to blow out the step and slide downhill, so stay upright. Weight your foot and bring up your downhill leg to kick in your next step.

Don't try to take gigantic steps. The people behind you—especially those shorter than you—won't thank you, and it requires extra energy to make a high step, so keep your steps even and relatively close together.

If you are following in a soft boot pack, you can enhance the trail by kicking in the steps a bit deeper as you ascend.

Use your poles for balance, although you can push down on them to assist you as you move up. It helps to plant your poles behind your butt to keep your weight upright and over your feet.

Mountaineers advocate moving one point at a time so you always maintain three points of contact. That means keeping one foot and both poles in place while you move the other foot, or moving one pole while your feet and the other pole stay stationary. You can also use the rest step to help conserve energy.

Carrying Your Skis

Your backpack will determine the best way to carry your skis on a boot pack. Some packs are designed to have the skis strapped together, base to base, and attached to the pack at an angle. Others are set up so you have a ski attached to straps on either side of the pack. Most people then use a ski strap to pull the tips together so your skis form an A-shape. Either technique works

There are two basic styles for attaching skis to a backpack: either bases together across the back of your pack at an angle or in an A-shape along the sides of the pack.

fine—just make sure your skis are centered so they aren't too high and top heavy or so low the tails drag in the snow or hit your calves as you hike.

Transitions

A big part of AT touring is making the transition from hiking to skiing or vice versa as efficiently as possible. For ski-mountaineering racers, transitions are key to their success; for recreational skiers, they are less critical, but good transitions save you time over the course of the day. Think about it: If every time you need a drink of water, it takes you half an hour to find your bottle and have a drink, you eat up lots of time that you could be using to move or ski over the course of the day. So it's important to be efficient.

Transitions include the following considerations:

- skins on or off
- bindings in ski or touring mode
- layers appropriate for climbing, skiing, or resting
- goggles or glasses on or off
- refueling with food and water

You need to anticipate all these different steps as you pull into your rest stop. If you just collapse on your pack in exhaustion, you're likely to get cold and waste time.

Pick a good spot for your transitions. You don't want to stop in the middle of a steep slope where a mitten can tumble downhill if you put it down in the wrong place or, worse, where you are exposed to avalanche danger. Likewise, it's nice to get out of the wind and have shelter if it's stormy. When you pull into a rest stop, put on extra layers right away to trap all that heat you've generated while climbing. That includes a hat. Stay warm while you go through the transition.

It's important to stay organized. Don't explode all your gear out of your backpack. Not only will it get covered in snow, it's also easy to lose either in the powder or down the hill. Keep track of your equipment. You are carrying it for a reason. Losing anything could be dangerous in the winter.

Practice performing all your tasks in gloves or mittens. Mittens and gloves protect your skin from the cold and prevent frostbite or other cold injuries.

Putting Skins On and Taking Skins Off

Whether you are putting skins on or taking them off, work with one ski at a time, keeping the other one on your foot and planted in the snow. If you take off both skis in deep snow, you'll find yourself wallowing around. Plus you are less likely to accidentally drop a ski and lose it downhill if it is attached to your foot.

Stomp out a level platform. If you are putting your skins on, pull one out of your pack, leaving the other tucked away until you need it. Put the skin on your ski and then click back into your binding, making sure to swing your foot

Fold your skins together glue side in and stash them in your pack for the downhill.

back and forth to ensure the binding is secure. Then repeat the process on your other ski. In steep terrain you may feel more comfortable turning around so that you are standing on your downhill foot while putting the skin on your uphill ski.

If you are pulling off your skins, practice removing them without taking off your skis. Fold the skins together glue side in and stash them in your pack.

If you are skiing, lock down your heels, buckle your boots, switch them into ski mode, layer up, put on your goggles and your hat or helmet, eat some food, drink some water, and you are good to go. If you are skinning, strip off layers, loosen your boots, free your heels, eat some food, drink some water, and you are good to go.

You can use your backpack for a seat and your skis make a great backrest if you plan to take a long break. Jam the tails of your ski into the snow at a roughly 75-degree angle to support yourself as you lounge back in the sun for lunch.

CHAPTER 3

Backcountry Safety

The number-one concern for most of us in the backcountry is avalanches, but in reality there are other hazards we need to be prepared for when we head out into the winter on skis. Chapter 4 talks about avalanches. This chapter focuses on other environmental hazards relating to alpine touring.

Snow Immersion Suffocation

According to DeepSnowSafety.org, you are as statistically likely to suffocate in a tree well or in soft snow as you are in an avalanche, and yet many of us

To avoid tree wells, train your focus on the space between the trees rather than at the trees themselves since we tend to veer toward the things we look at. ALLEN O'BANNON

never think about that hazard. Tree wells are deep cavities that form around the base of a tree. The problem occurs when skiers fall headfirst into the hole and are unable to extricate themselves. Experiments reveal that 90 percent of those trapped in tree wells can't get out on their own, so this is a very real hazard.

The best precaution against snow immersion suffocation is to avoid tree wells. Sounds easy, but according to statistics the people who get trapped are advanced or expert skiers, so even the best athletes get caught if they aren't careful. To avoid tree wells, focus on the spaces between the trees as you ski. Just like driving a car, if you stare at an object, you are likely to head right toward it, so look between the trees rather than at them.

Stay close to your partner in the trees. Use a radio to communicate or maintain visual contact. If your buddy goes in, you can't help him if you are 100 feet downhill. By the time you make it back up to him, it may be too late. People suffocate in snow as quickly as they drown, so time is of the essence. If you do see your friend inverted in a tree well, move downhill of the tree and let gravity assist you in pulling away snow and extricating your partner. Your goal is to ensure he or she has a clear airway first and then to get them out of the tree well.

If you find yourself heading for a tree well, do everything you can to avoid falling in upside down. Grab at branches or at the tree trunk. Roll so your skis go in first. Fight to stay upright. If your efforts are to no avail, don't panic. Struggling makes more snow fall in around you. Try to stay calm and to create an air pocket by slowly moving snow away from your face. Unlike avalanche debris, this snow is loose and unconsolidated so you should be able to move it, but if you move too quickly, more snow will fall in around you. If you can feel the tree, try to use it to help you get upright. Kick off your skis. If you have a cell phone or radio, call for help.

Cold Injuries

Part of the allure of winter is that it is cold and snowy. But humans aren't well adapted to cold temperatures. We don't have fur, and we don't (hopefully) build up a layer of insulating fat every autumn. Instead we need to use our brains to adapt.

Humans are designed to function best within a narrow body temperature range, roughly a degree or so on either side of 98.6 degrees Fahrenheit. Moving away from that norm in either direction can be dangerous, even life-threatening. In the winter our primary concern is staying warm enough.

We lose heat through the following ways:

- Conduction (the transfer of heat through direct contact between a cold body and a warm one), which is what happens when you sit on the snow with no insulating pad separating you from its chill.

- Convection (the loss of heat to moving water or air). The rate of convection depends on the difference between your temperature and the temperature of the moving air or water. That difference is pretty extreme in the winter when air temperatures are usually below freezing. Wind speed adds to the chilling effect of convection. It feels a lot colder out there when the wind is blowing 20 mph than it does when the air is calm.

- Radiation (the heat our bodies give off as a by-product of our basic metabolism). We lose up to 65 percent of our body heat through radiation. It's usually a good way to keep us from overheating, but it can be problematic when we are out in the winter.

- Evaporation (the loss of heat from moisture—usually sweat—evaporating off our skin). A wet surface loses heat as much as twenty-five times faster than a dry one. This is great in the summer when you are hot and need to cool down, but it can be deadly in the winter.

Our goal in the winter is to maintain a comfortable body temperature. At times that means minimizing heat loss, at other times it means maximizing it. You don't want to get too sweaty out there, nor do you want to get overly chilled. To maintain that happy medium, you need to constantly add and shed layers of clothing. Think about the type of layers you are wearing and how they protect against heat loss. A wind shirt will stop convective heat loss by blocking out the wind, while a down jacket traps the heat you are radiating off in the dead air space of its insulation.

That said, most of us have experienced getting too cold at least once in our lives. If you spend a lot of time out in the winter, it's hard not to. Mild hypothermia—or too little heat—can be treated easily if you recognize the symptoms. That's where it should stop. Moderate hypothermia takes more aggressive efforts to reverse, while severe hypothermia can be deadly.

Hypothermia

Hypothermia usually shows up as a kind of gradual deterioration. As you get colder, your symptoms become more obvious and more incapacitating, so it's critical to recognize what's happening early and to take action to stop it quickly.

Some people describe these symptoms as the "umbles." As a person's core temperature drops, he or she begins to bumble, stumble, grumble, and mumble. Initially this may mean you have trouble zipping your jacket or performing other fine motor skills. You feel cold and may be shivering. As things get worse, your gross motor skills become affected and you may have trouble

To avoid hypothermia, pay attention to your body temperature and keep an eye on your partners when you are out in stormy conditions. ALLEN O'BANNON

walking. You may become grumpy or apathetic and find it hard to speak normally. As you slide from mild to moderate hypothermia, your level of consciousness deteriorates, and you may answer questions inappropriately or be confused about where you are and what is happening.

Sometimes it's easier to recognize these changes in someone other than yourself. So keep an eye on your teammates when you are out in stormy conditions, and if you see them display any sign of the umbles, stop and do something about it.

The end of this spectrum is losing consciousness and becoming unresponsive. Don't get there.

Treatment for Mild to Moderate Hypothermia

When you first begin to detect signs that you are getting too cold, it's pretty easy to reverse the progression. Your goal is to get warm. Exercise ups our heat generation by as much as fifteen to eighteen times. So if you feel chilled, do fifty jumping jacks, run around, swing your arms or legs, or go for a ski to get your blood flowing and your furnace kicking.

It's also a good idea to get out of the offending environment either by moving into a protected spot or adding layers to help prevent heat loss. If you

Add layers when you stop to rest so you don't get cold. It's easier to stay warm than it is to get warm after you are cold.

are wet, get into dry clothes. If it's blowing, put on a wind shirt or find some shelter. Drink something warm and eat something to restore your energy.

With more moderate hypothermia, people tend to get increasingly apathetic. You may just feel like sitting down and cuddling up in a ball. You may begin to be increasingly incoherent and slow to respond to questions. As you get colder, you may lose your coordination and be unable to walk without falling. These are not good signs.

When someone is moderately cold, start your treatment by making sure he or she is in warm, dry clothes and out of the elements. If the individual is capable of drinking from a cup by herself, give her warm fluids and a snack. If the person shows no signs of improvement after these initial steps, you'll need to be more aggressive in your treatment.

When you are camping, you can make a hypothermic wrap with a tarp, sleeping bag, pad, and hot water bottles to treat a moderately hypothermic person, but on most day tours you won't have that gear with you. Instead, dress the person as warmly as possible, making sure to protect him from conductive and convective heat loss. If the individual is capable of skiing, get him moving toward the road. If he cannot move on his own, you may need to go for help. Obviously it's better not to let anyone get to this point.

If your patient is severely hypothermic, gently wrap him up in as many layers as possible. Take care not to be too jarring or rough in your handling of the patient, as sudden movements can cause heart problems in a severely cold human. The layers will not rewarm this person, but they can help prevent further heat loss. Go for help. This individual will need medical attention, but even if he appears dead, there is hope. Some severely hypothermic people are successfully rewarmed.

Frostbite

Frostbite happens when your body tissue freezes, generally on your extremities or in exposed spots like your nose or ears because your body shunts blood away from these areas to protect your more important core and brain. Frostbite can be very serious and cause loss of fingers and toes and other bits and pieces, so you really want to avoid it.

Frostbite is evaluated like a burn: superficial, partial thickness, and full thickness. The thickness refers to your skin tissue. Superficial frostbite just affects the top layer of skin, partial thickness goes deeper, and full-thickness frostbite freezes through the skin layer into your subcutaneous fat.

To help prevent frostbite, avoid wearing constricting clothing or too-tight boots to ensure you have good circulation. Make sure to stay hydrated and don't tolerate cold feet or hands. If your toes or fingers feel numb, stop and do something about it. Swing your legs and arms, do jumping jacks . . . anything to force blood into your cold parts. If your feet don't seem to be rewarming through exercise, ask a friend if you can put them on his or her stomach. It can be brutal to have cold feet touch your warm belly, but it's an effective way to warm them up.

There are situations—say a long, difficult peak ascent or when you are caught out in severe weather—when all your preventative measures fail and you end up with frozen toes, fingers, or facial parts.

The mildest form of frostbite—superficial frostbite—generally presents as a white spot on your cheek or nose. Usually these spots disappear immediately if you put your hands to your face and blow warm air into the pocket formed between your palms. Make sure to check one another's faces when you are out in cold, windy conditions, because you may not feel the spots on your own skin. After you rewarm your skin, cover exposed areas to prevent frostnip from occurring again.

Partial- and full-thickness frostbite are a lot more serious, and they look pretty much the same at first. The affected area will be white and hard to the touch. Full-thickness frostbite may feel stiffer, but you probably won't be able to tell the difference. And if your toes or fingers are frozen, it doesn't matter how frozen they are in terms of how you respond in the field.

The treatment for frostbite is to rewarm the part in a bath of water between 98.6 and 102 degrees Fahrenheit until it is thawed. Practically,

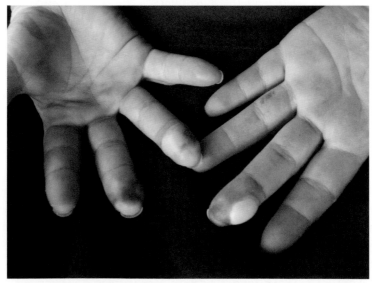

Partial-thickness frostbite causes blisters to form after the area is rewarmed.
Dave Anderson

however, you are not going to be able to do that when you are out on a ski tour. In this case, your best bet is to try to thaw the frozen part through skin-to-skin contact. Put your hand on your belly or your foot on your friend's stomach and let that body warmth thaw them out.

The process can be extremely painful. Climbers often say thawing hands cause them to experience the "screaming barfies," and if you've ever felt the sensation of blood returning to cold parts, you'll understand the saying. It hurts. So plan to take some painkillers. Ibuprofen in conjunction with Tylenol can be as effective as narcotics in treating pain. Take the highest recommended dose of each medication together or, better yet, stagger them every 4 hours.

We used to talk about trying to keep a frostbitten hand or foot frozen while you evacuated to prevent repeated freezing and thawing. Evidence has shown this to be impractical, however. If you are exercising, it's likely the limb will thaw regardless of your efforts to keep it frozen. Warm the area skin-to-skin and get out of the mountains as rapidly as possible. There's been a lot of progress made in the treatment of frostbite that's saving more and more tissue, so it's worth seeking care from a physician experienced with frostbite to ensure you get the best outcome possible.

Raynaud's Syndrome

Raynaud's syndrome is a condition that causes the arteries that supply blood to your skin to spasm in response to cold temperatures and stress. Typically,

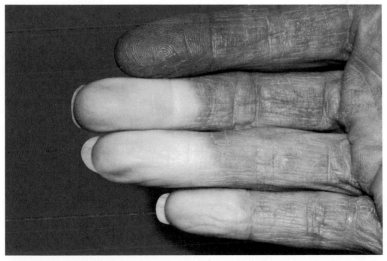

Raynaud's syndrome causes the blood vessels in your skin to spasm, limiting circulation to the affected area. TWINSCHOICE

Raynaud's affects people's fingers or toes. The skin usually turns pale or white, then blue during these spasms. The affected area will feel numb and cold, and your sense of touch may be dulled. As the spasms subside and circulation improves, the area may turn red and throb or tingle.

Raynaud's is usually more of a nuisance than a disability. Many people know they have Raynaud's before they head out into the winter and so have developed tricks for dealing with the problem, such as wearing insulated mittens or heavy socks, carrying chemical hand and foot warmers, and taking care to stay warm and dry. If you experience an attack of Raynaud's in the field, warm the affected area gently until the spasms subside and circulation improves.

Snow Blindness and Sunburn

Snow reflects light, intensifying the power of the sun. It's easy to get a sunburn in the winter even on an overcast day because of this. In addition, you can burn your corneas, causing snow blindness. Snow blindness is quite painful. It feels like you have sand in your eyes. Often you can't do much more than sit in a dark room with cold compresses on your eyes until the symptoms go away, which usually takes about 24 hours. The key, therefore, is to avoid a burn. Wear glasses or goggles with UV protection and be sure to use sunscreen on your face and lip balm with sun protection on your lips.

Environmental Hazards

Chapter 4 tackles the complex subject of avalanches, but there are other environmental hazards an alpine ski tourer should be aware of, namely extreme weather and ice or open water.

Extreme weather can turn a pleasant ski tour deadly very quickly. Cold temperatures made worse by high winds threaten our ability to stay warm. Blowing snow and low clouds reduce visibility, leaving you disoriented and unable to make your way out of the backcountry to safety. Mountaineers say being in a whiteout is like being on the inside of a Ping-Pong ball. It's hard to tell up from down and all too easy to find yourself walking in circles when everything around you is white.

Getting lost in the winter can be life-threatening if you do not have the appropriate gear to stay comfortable in cold temperatures. If you find yourself unable to see the landscape to navigate and you don't have tracks to follow, your best bet is to put on your warm clothes and hunker down to wait until conditions improve. Wandering around aimlessly in a whiteout is rarely effective unless you have a compass or GPS to point the way.

Digging down into the snow to create an emergency shelter can help protect you from the elements if you get stranded in a storm. ALLEN O'BANNON

You can build an emergency shelter to get out of the elements if you find yourself stranded by the weather. The simplest shelter is either a trench or a snow cave.

Dig a trench deep enough for you to crouch down or sit on your pack inside. Cover the opening with branches or place skis across the top and spread a tarp or wind jacket over the skis and pile snow on top to create a kind of roof. If you have a snow saw in your backpack, you can cut blocks out of wind-packed snow to cover your trench. Lean the blocks in from opposite sides to create a V-shaped roof overhead. Once your trench is closed in, get inside and sit or lie down on your backpack to keep off the snow.

If you find a snowdrift, you can hollow into it to make a cave. It doesn't have to be big, just something to protect you from the storm while you wait for conditions to improve. To build a snow cave, hollow out a chamber with an arcing roof to create a dome-shaped cavity where you can hang out. Ideally have one person stand by the door to move snow away while another excavates the cave.

Ice and open water can be tricky to evaluate in the winter. At times skiing across a flat, frozen lake is the quickest, safest route to get to a given destination. But early in the season or in the spring when things are starting to melt out, frozen lakes and rivers can be hazardous.

Skiing across a frozen lake can be a quick way to reach your destination, but you need to evaluate the ice to ensure it can support your weight. PETER ABSOLON

Ice must be at least 3 inches thick to support the weight of a skier. It can be hard to tell how thick that is, but if you tap ice with your ski pole and it gives a solid *thunk*, it's usually safe, especially if conditions have consistently been cold.

Snow-covered ice needs to be evaluated before you forge across it unless it's midwinter and the temperatures have stayed below freezing for weeks. Snow provides insulation and may prevent the water from freezing thickly enough to support your weight, so if a lake is snow-covered, clear some of it aside to assess the integrity of the ice beneath it.

Ice tends to be thinner and less consistent in areas of moving water, and it melts out faster near rocks or logs or at the inlets and outlets of a lake. Try to avoid such areas.

Snow bridges often form over creeks and rivers and can make good crossings for skiers. Try to evaluate the bridge from the side to make sure it is thick enough to support your weight.

Snow bridges often thin out in the middle making them dangerous to cross. Your weight is spread out on your skis, which is an asset when crossing dubious bridges or short sections of thin ice, but you don't want to be taken

The best stream crossings are found where logs have fallen down across a creek and become covered with a thick layer of snow.

by surprise. The best bridges form where logs or brush have fallen across the stream, allowing snow to build up.

If you break through and are submerged in water, you'll instantly feel a rush of panic. That's a normal response that will pass. Give yourself a minute to calm your breath and relax, then try to get out of the water. You will

Snow bridges tend to thin out in the middle so be sure to evaluate their thickness before you commit to crossing one.

probably need to take your skis off to get out if the water is deep. If you can pull your leg up to release the binding without losing your ski, great. Push the skis up onto the ice so you can use them later. They may be critical for getting out of the mountains. If you can't get your skis out of the water, better to lose them than to drown.

Once your skis are off, lay your arms across the ice, pushing them out as far as possible in front of you. Your feet will probably be hanging directly below you. Kick them back into a horizontal position, feet close to the surface. Then kick hard trying to propel your body forward and up onto the ice. If you are successful, don't stand up. Remember, that ice just broke through on you. Crawl forward, keeping your body as flat as possible until you are confident you've reached safety. If you have dry clothes, change. If you don't, wring out what you have, put everything back on, and start skiing back to your car as quickly as possible.

You have about 10 minutes of effective movement in freezing water before your body chills down and you lose your muscle coordination and strength, so fight hard while you can to get yourself out of the water.

If you cannot get out on your own, stretch your arms out in front of you across the ice. You probably have close to an hour before you will lose consciousness, so try to hang on until someone comes to help. Even if you pass out, you may still be rescued if your arms freeze in place, keeping you from sinking underwater.

In the best-case scenario, you will not be alone when you fall through. Your colleagues can help you, but they need to make sure they don't make the situation worse by falling through themselves. The best way to rescue someone who has broken through ice is to throw him a rope or to push a ski, log, stick, or some strong, long object out to him to grab on to. Stay well away from the hole in the ice.

If you have a rope, make a loop in the end that your partner can slide over his head and shoulders, hooking it in his armpits so you can pull him out. If you have to use a stick or pole, make sure there is something for your partner to hang on to. If it's too slippery, he won't be able to maintain a grip while being pulled out of the water.

Once your partner is out, help him wring out his clothes or get into something dry and get moving. Exercise will be the best way for him to get warm in the backcountry after a dunk in icy water.

Avalanches

Avalanches Are Wicked

Winter snowpack is complex and varied. Every season creates its own unique snowpack, and every location has its own idiosyncrasies. This makes understanding avalanches hard. People dedicate their lives to studying snow slides, and still, occasionally even these experts get caught. It's just that hard to understand everything that goes into making a slope safe or unsafe, and you don't always know if you made the right call or just got lucky.

Sociologists lump learning into "wicked" and "kind" environments. Kind environments give you immediate and specific feedback that enables you to

Avalanches are complex and dangerous. If you want to tour in the backcountry, you need to understand the hazard. JOHN FITZGERALD

learn from your mistakes without dire consequences. Wicked environments do not. Avalanches are wicked.

Wicked environments provide incomplete feedback and allow you to get off scot-free if you are lucky or can kill you if you are not. The classic example of a wicked environment is when you get behind the wheel of a car. Most of the time you drive without encountering any problems, despite knowing rationally that the risks are high. Driving feels easy so it's hard for people to really believe that it is dangerous. Or if they do acknowledge the risks, they convince themselves that they are such good drivers they can avoid the hazards.

Avalanches are similar. We know the slopes we ski in the backcountry can slide. The signs are obvious: Some of our best runs are down funnel-shaped gullies lined with flagged trees that scream to us of past avalanches, but most of the time we ski past these indicators without any problems. This experience leaves us with the belief that we know what we are doing and that we made a good decision, which in turn encourages us to trust our instincts and experience and to use that information for future decision making. But the reality is that unless we make a bad decision and suffer the consequences, we'll never know if we were smart or just lucky.

Often the slopes we ski in the backcountry show obvious signs of past slides like the unhappy forest at the bottom of this run. ANDREW MORLEY

Whitewater boating, on the other hand, is an example of a kind environment. You learn your weaknesses quickly when you enter a rapid without the necessary skills, and because of this, most people up the difficulty of the water they attempt slowly, giving themselves time to get comfortable with a lower grade before they try something harder. They know that if they are swimming in Class II rapids, they have no business attempting a Class IV.

Unfortunately, backcountry skiing has no such learning curve. We don't routinely go out and test ourselves in an easy avalanche to gain skills for dealing with the big one. There is no such thing as an easy avalanche, which means backcountry skiers don't know how many times they've lucked out in their choices because they don't experience any feedback until they blow it.

That doesn't mean we shouldn't learn about avalanches and do our best to make careful decisions about the slopes we ski. We should. But it does mean we should always recognize that we are fallible, and a clean track record is no guarantee we've made good decisions.

This book cannot replace an avalanche course that includes time in the field with experts. Learning about snow requires looking at it, feeling it,

Learning about snow requires looking at it, feeling it, conducting tests, and watching for patterns. Your best way to learn these skills is to take an avalanche course taught by the experts.

conducting tests, and watching for patterns. What this book can do is help you learn to identify avalanche terrain and introduce you to the tools you can use to determine if avalanches are possible. You can pick up enough information here to make the easy decisions when the hazard is either very low or very high, but most of the time, conditions are not that black-and-white. It's the gray areas that require experience, education, and mentoring. If you really plan to spend time touring in steep, snow-covered terrain, you need to take an avalanche class and to travel with people who know more than you.

The Basics

An avalanche is a sudden flow of snow down a slope that occurs when a trigger—either a natural trigger like new snow or an artificial trigger like a skier—overloads the strength of the bonds holding the snowpack in place. There are two main categories of snow slides: sluffs and slab avalanches.

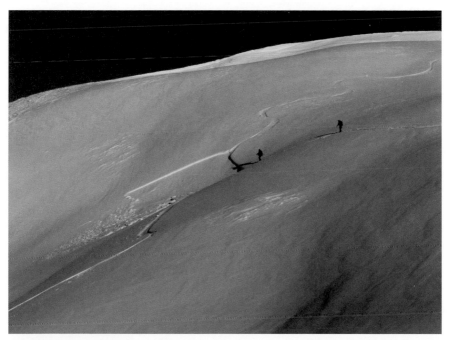

An avalanche is a sudden flow of snow down a slope after a trigger—in this case a skier—overloads the strength of the bonds holding the snowpack in place. JOHN FITZGERALD

Sluffs

Sluffs occur when the top layer of loose, powdery snow slides. Sluffs, which are also called point-release slides, start from a single point, entraining more snow as they flow downhill to form a characteristic teardrop shape. Skiers on slopes steeper than 40 degrees often trigger sluffs.

Sluffs occur when the top layer of loose, powdery snow slides. DON SHARAF

Sluffs generally do not pile up deeply enough to cause burial, but they can knock you off your feet and carry you, which can be dangerous. You can manage a sluff by traversing back and forth across a slope out of the moving snow, but that isn't very fun if you are out to make turns. Some skiers are good enough to out-ski their sluffs, but if you don't have confidence in your ability to do that, you are better off making a few turns and stopping to wait for the moving snow to pass. Another trick is to angle your track laterally across the slope, moving away from flowing snow with each turn in what looks like a set of stairs. You'll need a fairly big slope for this technique to work effectively.

Slabs

The deadliest avalanches are slab avalanches. These occur when the bonds within a layer of snow or slab are stronger than the bonds between that layer and the snow below. Slabs become a problem when they lie on a weak layer above a sliding layer. In this configuration, it may not take much to trigger the weak layer to collapse and the slab to fail.

The angle at which most slab avalanches occur is between 30 and 50 degrees, with 35 to 40 degrees being the most common range (38 degrees is considered prime time).

Slab avalanches release as one cohesive unit along the crown line and then slide downhill, entraining more snow as they run. JOHN FITZGERALD

Slab avalanches are categorized as wet or cold, hard or soft. Wet slides are common in the spring, especially if temperatures stay above freezing overnight, and can occur on slopes of less than 30 degrees. Cold slabs form in the winter as a result of storm cycles, droughts, warming trends, cold snaps, wind, and sun. All of these factors affect the character of the snowpack and can create conditions where dangerous hard or soft slabs can form.

If you could watch a slab avalanche in slow motion, you'd see that it releases as one cohesive unit at what's called the crown, which usually runs along the rollover of a slope where the downward pull is greatest. That block of snow slides downhill, leaving distinctive flanks on either side and breaking up into blocks and chunks as it careens down the avalanche track. Dry slab avalanches reach speeds of 60 to 80 mph within 5 seconds.

Avalanche Triangle

Doug Fesler and Jill Fredson came up with the idea of the avalanche triangle back in 1984, and it continues to be the most popular framework for thinking about avalanches. Their triangle has "weather", "snowpack", and "terrain" on each side, with a skier—the human factor—in the middle. These are the factors that contribute to the risk of an avalanche.

Terrain

Slope Angle

For new alpine tourers, terrain is the number-one consideration. Avalanche terrain is the easiest thing for beginners to identify and, therefore, to avoid.

As mentioned earlier, slopes over 30 degrees are suspect unless it's spring and the temperatures are warm—then you need to expand that range down to 25 or so. How do you know what a 30-degree slope looks like? The best way to measure the slope angle is to use an inclinometer. You can try to guess, but it's likely your guess will be wrong, and being off by a degree or two can be significant. Nowadays, you can get an app for your smartphone that allows you to measure slope angle. To ensure accuracy, lay your ski pole along the fall line and place your inclinometer on the pole to take your reading.

Take time to measure the slopes you ski so you start to get a feel for steepness. Remember, black diamond or expert runs at most ski areas start around 30 degrees, so if the slope you want to ski looks like an expert run, it's probably steep enough to slide.

The easiest way to avoid avalanches is to ski slopes of less than 30 degrees. JOHN FITZGERALD

Slope Aspect

The direction a slope faces, or its aspect, affects the quality of the snow you'll find. A south-facing slope gets more sun, so the snow is warmer. That can lead to a stronger snowpack as the snow crystals generally bond together under warmer conditions. But south-facing slopes also tend to form sun crusts that can become sliding layers if they get buried beneath a cohesive slab. South-facing slopes can also warm up fast in the spring, resulting in wet slides.

North-facing slopes often have sugary, unconsolidated snow and thinner snowpacks. In general, north-facing slopes are more dangerous because of this. Sugary, faceted snow forms a weak layer that can be dangerous when buried.

Terrain Traps

Small slopes can produce an avalanche. Sometimes these slides are innocuous because they don't entrain enough snow to bury you, but If they flow into a steep-sided gully, even a tiny avalanche can be deadly. Gullies force snow to pile up and can bury skiers. So be aware of the runout of any slope you ski. A terrain trap at the bottom adds to the consequences of a slide.

Some terrain traps are obvious, like the gully at the bottom of these avalanche paths. If a slide came down while you were in this gully, you'd be toast. Other terrain traps are subtler. A small slide can pile up quickly in a creek bed or gully, burying you deeply. LYNNE WOLFE

Terrain Clues

Mother Nature leaves behind clues that indicate if a slope is prone to avalanches. Look for "unhappy forests" or small trees that haven't had a chance to grow tall because they get pruned by frequent slides. Another sign is a slope covered with flexible shrubs like alders and willows that bend rather than break when avalanches flow over them.

But don't assume tall trees mean a slope can't slide. Skiers often say you know a treed slope is safe from avalanches if the forest is too thick to ski through. Slopes with widely spaced trees can and do slide. You may be able to tell by looking closely at the trees. Often trees on avalanche slopes will only have branches on the downhill side of their trunks or the trees will be bent or broken. But don't count on obvious clues.

Pay attention to the signs, and if you don't want to get into avalanche terrain, avoid any slope that exhibits them. If you want to ski a slope and you see these signs, you need to assess the snow conditions before venturing onto it.

Categorizing Terrain

Canadian avalanche forecasters use an avalanche-exposure scale to categorize terrain.

- Simple terrain is low-angle, mostly forested, rolling or flat. You may encounter runout zones to an infrequent avalanche path in simple terrain, but there are easy ways to avoid it. Simple terrain is where you want to be when the hazard is high or you are a novice and do not have the skills to evaluate avalanche conditions.

- Challenging terrain has exposure to well-defined avalanche paths, starting zones, and terrain traps. You can reduce or avoid exposure to these hazards with careful route finding, but you need skill and experience to recognize the danger.

- Complex terrain has exposure to multiple, overlapping avalanche paths or large expanses of steep, open terrain with multiple avalanche starting zones and terrain traps. Complex terrain has very few or no options to reduce or avoid exposure.

This scale is helpful when used in conjunction with other factors. For example, if you know it hasn't snowed in two weeks and the avalanche hazard is low, you may choose to venture into complex terrain. If the hazard is high and you just got a 2-foot dump, you probably want to stay in simple terrain.

When you go to the alpine zone to ski, you are usually entering complex terrain where it is impossible to avoid avalanche paths. Be cautious and enter this type of terrain only when you are confident in the snow's stability. JOHN FITZGERALD

Weather

Weather is what makes and changes the snowpack. It adds and subtracts snow; it changes the quality and strength of snow, it moves it, warms it, and melts it. Every weather change makes something happen in the snowpack. The question to ask yourself is: Is that change making the snow stronger or weaker?

Past Weather

Past weather is all the stuff that's buried beneath your skis as you head up into the mountains. It's the rainstorm that left an ice crust 6 inches off the ground

Stop and dig hasty pits as you tour to get a sense of what is happening in the snow around you.

Check for avalanche conditions, weather information, and snow observations at regional avalanche-information sites like this one for the Colorado Avalanche Information Center.

in January, or the cold, dry snap in February that created a layer of surface hoar that is now buried. It's the warm spell when the snowpack consolidated and a sun crust formed on south-facing slopes. And it's that 12-inch dump of snow you got last week that is slowly settling out.

You can find this information by digging a snowpit and examining the layers, but sometimes things can be subtle, so it helps to have an idea of what you should be looking for. A lot of people who live and ski in a particular mountainous area keep a weather log throughout the winter beginning with the first snowfall that sticks around. That way they can predict what is happening to the snow even if they haven't been able to get out to dig for a few days.

If you are a visitor to an area, you have a few choices. A good place to start is the avalanche-forecasting website for the region. These sites often have a weather archive that will allow you to look back at the season's data. You can also talk to the locals about what's been happening and what to look for in the snow. And, most importantly, you can dig a lot of pits. After a while you'll begin to recognize some of the layers that show up throughout the snowpack.

Current Weather

Current weather is what is happening now when you step out of your car and put on your skis. The primary things to consider with the current weather are: precipitation, temperature, and wind.

Begin making your weather observations in the car on the way to your ski day. You can tell a lot about conditions by what you see through your windshield.

Most avalanches occur during snowstorms as a natural way for a slope to restore balance after it has been overloaded. How much snow this takes depends. In general, your warning lights should go off if snow is falling at more than 1 inch per hour for 6 hours or if you get more than 12 inches in 24 hours. That doesn't automatically mean avalanche hazard will be high after such a storm—dry, fluffy powder may not overload the snowpack—but the potential for avalanches goes up when you get a big dump.

Snow accumulation doesn't only occur during a blizzard. High winds can move snow and load a slope just as effectively as a storm. Winds stronger than 20 mph transport huge amounts of snow and so should be a red flag for ski tourers.

Temperature affects the kind of snow that accumulates during a storm. Cold snow is typically lighter and fluffier and less dangerous, while a warm, wet storm will be heavy and can load the snowpack quickly. The best scenario is a storm that comes in warm and gets colder. That results in light snow on top of heavy. When a storm comes in cold and gets warm, you get what's called an upside-down snowpack. The problem here is that you have a potential slab of new heavy snow on top of a weaker layer, which can create dangerous sliding conditions.

Finally, watch the temperature as you tour. Rapidly warming temperatures can be problematic as they can increase the load on the snowpack, again pushing it past a tipping point of its strength and creating unstable conditions in the snowpack. Slow warming is OK, especially if that warming doesn't approach freezing. Slow warming can strengthen the snowpack, but when the sun beats down and the trees begin to drip, watch out and pay attention.

Snowpack

Truly understanding the layers in a snowpack is the most complicated part of avalanche forecasting. You can take temperatures, perform stress tests, and document layers in your analysis and still be left with questions. The best way to learn to understand the snowpack is to dig a lot of pits with guidance from someone who has more experience than you to help you interpret your findings.

Simply speaking, snow changes, or metamorphoses, once it hits the ground. When temperatures are warm (and we're talking winter warm, so upper teens and low to mid-20s), the crystals round out and form necks between the individual grains, creating a strong bond that holds the snowpack together. That's good as long as the well-bonded snow doesn't lie on

If you really want to learn about the snowpack, you need to dig a lot of pits and examine the snow closely. JOHN FITZGERALD

top of a weak layer above a sliding surface. Then you have a recipe for an avalanche.

In cold temperatures snow crystals become faceted or angled, and the bonds between grains break down, creating sugary weak snow. This often happens at the interface between the snow and the ground and is called

Surface hoar forms on the top of the snow during calm, clear periods. It can get especially big around creek beds or holes. Once it gets buried, surface hoar can be a dangerous weak layer.

Geographical Snowpack Variations

A maritime snowpack is influenced by its proximity to the ocean, which moderates the weather. Maritime snowpacks are generally deep (more than 3 meters on average) and made up of high-density snow (10 to 20 percent water by volume). Average winter temperatures are relatively warm, ranging between 23 and 41 degrees Fahrenheit. Wind layers are typically less pronounced than in other climates, and most avalanches occur during storms. Wet slides are possible throughout the season, and it's not uncommon to have rain in midwinter.

An intermountain snowpack is between 1.5 and 3 meters deep, and average winter temperatures are generally colder than close to the ocean (5 to 27 degrees Fahrenheit), meaning the snow is less dense. Instabilities can last longer in an intermountain snowpack than in maritime snow.

A continental snowpack is shallow (less than 1.5 meters), and the snow is often quite low-density. Average temperatures range between −22 and 14 degrees Fahrenheit, and persistent layers of depth hoar and surface hoar are common throughout the winter.

The boundaries between these snowpacks are fluid and can vary within a single mountain range, but it's useful to know the general characteristics of an area if, for example, you live in New England and are planning a ski trip in Colorado, which is known for its continental snowpack.

depth hoar. Depth hoar is common in shallow snowpacks and on north-facing slopes where temperatures tend to be colder. Depth hoar does not form a slab, so it's not inherently dangerous, but once it is buried by subsequent storms, it can be a dangerous weak layer, especially if it's on top of a good sliding surface like ice or the ground.

Snow also metamorphoses on the surface. The sun can warm it into a sun crust, or the wind can transform it into a well-bonded wind slab. Long cold snaps can cause near-surface faceting, resulting in a sugary weak layer that becomes dangerous if it gets buried in a subsequent storm. And during clear, still nights, feathery crystals known as surface hoar may grow. Surface hoar makes a lovely tinkling sound when you ski through it, but once it's buried, it's like a line of dominoes ready to fall over with a gentle touch.

What to Do with All This Information

It's good to establish habits for assessing the avalanche hazard. Those habits begin when you check the avalanche forecast for the area each morning before you head out for your tour. Most people pull up the local forecasting center's website to see what the experts have to say about what's going on in the mountains. You can also call the avalanche hotline to listen to a recorded message.

An avalanche forecast includes information on the snowpack and the weather, both current weather and what is projected to occur over the next 24 hours. Most sites include a map showing recent avalanche activity (remember, not all slides are recorded), as well as other observations about

What the Hazard Ratings Mean

Danger Level	Travel Advice	Likelihood of Avalanches	Avalanche Size and Distribution
Extreme	Avoid all avalanche terrain	Natural and human-triggered avalanches certain	Large to very large avalanches in many areas
High	Very dangerous avalanche conditions; travel in avalanche terrain is not recommended	Natural avalanches likely; human-triggered avalanches very likely	Large avalanches in many areas or very large avalanches in specific areas
Considerable	Dangerous avalanche conditions; careful snowpack evaluation, cautious route finding, and conservative decision making essential	Natural avalanches possible; human-triggered avalanches likely	Small avalanches in many areas; large avalanches in specific areas, or very large avalanches in isolated areas
Moderate	Heightened avalanche conditions on specific terrain features; evaluate snow and terrain carefully and identify features of concern	Natural avalanches unlikely; human-triggered avalanches possible	Small avalanches in isolated areas or extreme terrain
Low	Generally safe avalanche conditions; watch for unstable snow on isolated terrain features	Natural and human-triggered avalanches unlikely	Small avalanches in isolated areas or extreme terrain

conditions. The forecast will then give you a hazard rating of low, moderate, considerable, high, or extreme. This is a general forecast and should not be the determining factor in your personal decision making, but it can be a good guide for helping you decide where to ski that day. If the forecast is high, you probably don't want to do a tour in complex terrain where avoiding slide paths is impossible.

Field Tests

Once you leave your house, start adding to the information you gathered from the avalanche forecast. Look, listen, and feel to get a sense of what is

To get a sense of what's happening beneath the snow's surface, push the handle of your ski pole down slowly, feeling for hard crusts or loose depth hoar.

going on. You can accumulate some data on the drive to the road head. Is the road wet or packed with new snow? Are your windshield wipers freezing up, or is the snow so dry you don't need wipers to keep your windshield clear?

Keep scanning your surroundings as you strap on your skis and start skinning. You are looking for how much new snow has fallen or for plumes of snow blowing off the high peaks and recent avalanche activity on surrounding slopes. Watch for cracks that shoot away as you break through the surface of the snow. When you make a kick turn, step above the skin track and stomp down on the snow to see if you can create a miniature slab. Keep a lookout for the telltale glitter of surface hoar on a meadow. All these signs tell you something.

You can feel for clues to conditions as well. Punch your pole down through the snow. Do you meet resistance? Does your pole get stuck and then fall down freely after you break through? Does the snow feel hollow underneath? Is the skin track slippery? Are you breaking trail? If so, what's the quality of the snow? Can you stay on top or are you dropping through?

Slab avalanches require a layer of cohesive snow lying on top of a weak layer above a sliding surface. Probing the snow and conducting tests allows you to feel for these factors. If you need to push hard to get your pole through

If you jump on the snow in a safe spot and it cracks and breaks into chunks, you know you have a dangerous slab. Stay off steep slopes in these conditions. JOHN FITZGERALD

ALPTRUTH

ALPTRUTH was developed by Ian McCammon to help guide decision making in avalanche terrain. Ian found that 92 percent of all avalanche accidents include at least three or more ALPTRUTH factors, which means if you see three ALPTRUTH factors on your tour, you know avalanches are likely.

A: Avalanches have occurred in the last 48 hours.

L: Loading has occurred in the last 48 hours (from snowfall or wind).

P: Path—an avalanche path is recognizable by a novice.

T: Terrain trap.

R: Rating by avalanche forecaster is considerable, high, or extreme.

U: Unstable snow (whumping, shooting cracks, collapsing, hollow sounds).

TH: Thaw instability or rapidly rewarming temperatures.

If you see three of the ALPTRUTH factors during your tour, such as recent avalanche activity, there's a high probability that more avalanches can occur. JOHN FITZGERALD

a firm layer before it drops into a void, you know you have a slab over a weak layer, which is cause for concern.

Do a few quick hand-shear tests as you skin. To do this, take the handle of your ski pole and cut out a square roughly 30 by 30 cm—or the size of your shovel blade—uphill of the skin track. Place your hand behind the back of the square and pull forward to see how well the top layer of snow is bonding to the layers below.

If you are traveling up a corniced ridge, you can drop parts of the cornice onto the slope below to test its strength. Pick a small cornice that you can see from the side so you know how far it projects over the slope. You don't want to be out on it if the entire thing collapses. Stand with one ski firmly above solid ground and stomp down on the cornice with your other foot to kick off chunks of snow. Watch to see how these bombs affect the slope below.

You can also listen for signs, the deadliest of which is the noise of collapsing snow. This sound—often described as "whomping" or "whumping"—is nature screaming at you that conditions are dangerous. It's the sound of the snowpack collapsing in response to your weight. That isn't a problem on a flat trail, but if the angle of the slope is right, it could trigger a slide.

Finally dig a pit to get a good sense of what is going on in the snowpack. This book does not go into how to dig a pit or conduct tests. There are lots of books on avalanches out there that go into great detail about analyzing snow. A good book to start with is *Allen & Mike's Avalanche Book* (Rowman & Littlefield, 2012) or Jill Fredston and Doug Fesler's *Snow Sense* (Alaska Mountain Safety Center Inc., 2011).

Human Factor

The bottom line in avalanches is that they are only dangerous if someone gets caught, so it's all about the human factor, really.

Unfortunately, humans aren't very good at making rational decisions. We let emotions and desire cloud our judgment, so even when we see signs of instability, we can talk ourselves out of concern because it's a beautiful day, there's 12 inches of fluffy untracked powder, and we only have today to ski. These are the kinds of things that get in the way of our really heeding the clues around us.

And it's not just desire that clouds our thinking. We may be tired, hungry, cold, or in a hurry. We may have paid lots of money to get where we are, and we have to leave the next day. We may have a friend who just skied the line, and we are jealous of his or her accomplishment. We may be showing off for a date. These are the subtle kinds of things that influence our decision making.

It can be hard to listen to your inner voice when there is untracked powder to ski.
JOHN FITZGERALD

So the challenge is to be honest and thorough and to recognize the factors that may be affecting our judgment. Studies have shown that having a checklist can help ensure that people don't miss obvious steps or signs in their decision making. So for ski tourers, it's probably a good idea to use the avalanche triangle (terrain, weather, and snowpack) and ALPTRUTH as a decision-making checklist before determining if a slope is safe to ski.

As you think about the snowpack, terrain, and weather, give each factor a red, green, or yellow light, meaning stop, go, or maybe. Obviously "maybe" will be the most challenging. If you find yourself facing yellow terrain, yellow snowpack, and yellow weather, it becomes pretty easy to decide that together that means red. But one yellow? Two?

One thing you can do to work around these hard choices is to conduct a pre-mortem. Ask yourself what the newspapers would say if you died in an avalanche on the slope. Did you miss some obvious clues? Would the article point to your ignorance or stupidity?

You should also consider how your death could affect others, especially your family and friends. Ultimately it's your decision to ski or not to ski, but you may not be the one who has to live with the consequences, so think about it.

Route Finding

A big part of staying safe in avalanche terrain is picking a good route that minimizes your exposure to danger. Stay out of steep-sided gullies and stick to low-angled slopes or heavily timbered areas. Avoid obvious slide paths. Know what is above you. Keep an eye on your partner and always know where he or she is. Consider carrying a radio so you can communicate when you are separated from the rest of your team. Don't travel below cornices and don't let yourself get boxed in where you have no way to escape without exposing yourself to danger.

Regardless of all these precautions, you can't always avoid avalanche slopes. You may have to cross an obvious path or you may want to ski one. First you must evaluate the snow conditions and weather to determine if you have a green light to proceed. Don't be afraid of turning around if you decide the situation is not safe. Respect the conservative voices in your party.

If you decide it's OK to move ahead, follow these guidelines to maximize your safety:

- Move one at a time, whether skiing or crossing an avalanche slope.

- Spot each other through exposed areas from islands of safety. Make a note of landmarks you can identify if an avalanche occurs and you need to know where your buddy was last seen.

- Move quickly and smoothly through exposed areas.

- Remove ski pole straps and unlock your skis so you don't have anchors attached to you in the event of a slide.

- Cross potential avalanche paths as high as possible and approach slopes from above so you can evaluate the hazard without being exposed.

If you decide an avalanche slope is safe to ski, you should still take precautions to minimize your exposure in case you make a bad call. Ski one at a time and spot each other from a safe area.

What to Do if You're Caught in an Avalanche

If you spend enough time skiing in avalanche terrain, at some point you, one of your partners, or someone you know may get caught in a slide. We want to do everything we can to avoid this eventuality, but given the fallibility of human decision making, we may not be able to, in which case it behooves us to know what to do when you blow the call.

If you happen to be the one caught, scream, "Avalanche," with all your might. Then point your skis at a 45-degree angle to the side of the slide and try to ski out. In a small slide you may succeed. More likely you will not. If you get knocked over, start fighting. Try to jettison your skis and poles. If you are wearing an airbag, deploy it. Put your Avalung in your mouth. Try to get on your back and swim to stay on top of the debris. If you find yourself getting sucked under, roll up like a ball to protect yourself and create an air pocket by burying your face into the crook of your elbow. Sounds easy, right? It's not. You may be moving at more than 60 mph and have little control over how the snow tosses and turns you, but it's worth trying to save yourself.

Avalanche debris sets up like cement, making it hard for rescuers to move through to find you. Avoid getting caught. JOHN FITZGERALD

As the snow slows, you may feel a change. If you can, thrust an arm upward in the hope it will break through the surface for others to see. Cover your mouth. Once the snow stops, relax. Most likely the snow will set up around you like cement, locking you into place and preventing any motion. Some soft slabs may be less confining, however. If you can move, work to clear space by your face and try to dig upward to the surface. Try not to panic. Save your air, remain calm, and wait patiently for your friends to find you.

If you are the one watching the slide, make a note of a landmark near where you last saw your buddy. When the slide stops, mark that point with a ski or pole or something so you know where it is. This will be the starting point for your search.

Avalanche Rescue

Rescue patterns are dictated by the size of your group. With any number, stop and survey the scene before you head out onto the slope. Make sure another avalanche won't come down on top of you. If you decide the coast is clear, take one more moment to look for clues like a ski or pole—or better yet a hand waving at you above the snow—before you dive into your beacon search.

Try to stay calm and to be methodical. If you panic, you are likely to make mistakes and prolong your search.

If you are alone, turn your transceiver to "Search" and begin moving back and forth across the slope below the last place you saw your buddy until you pick up the signal from his or her beacon. You may choose to do this part of your search with your skis on, but if the surface is firm and supports your weight, you may find it faster to move on foot. Your pattern should go back and forth in traversing lines approximately 40 meters apart and 20 meters from the edges of the slide path. Move quickly, listening for the beep and watching for a light.

Once you get a signal, follow the direction of the arrow on your transceiver, keeping an eye on the number. It should go down as you move closer to your friend. When the number reaches 20 meters, start slowing down, still following the direction arrow and homing in on the descending numbers. At 10 meters slow way down, moving only between beeps to ensure you don't miss anything.

At 3 meters stop, take off your skis if you haven't already, and begin your pinpoint search. Get down close to the snow. Move the beacon in a straight line away from you one beep at a time until you pass the loudest signal and smallest number. Move sideways from that loudest point in each direction to

Beacon Searching 101

There are three phases to an avalanche beacon search: the signal search, coarse search and fine search phases. It is essential to practice all three to become effective with your transceiver.

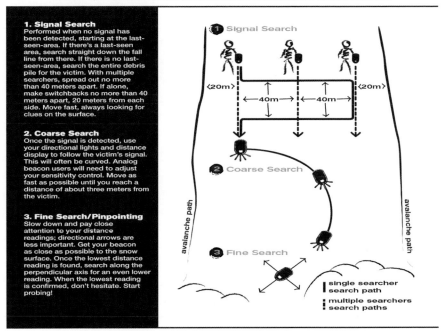

1. Signal Search
Performed when no signal has been detected, starting at the last-seen-area. If there's a last-seen area, search straight down the fall line from there. If there is no last-seen-area, search the entire debris pile for the victim. With multiple searchers, spread out no more than 40 meters apart. If alone, make switchbacks no more than 40 meters apart, 20 meters from each side. Move fast, always looking for clues on the surface.

2. Coarse Search
Once the signal is detected, use your directional lights and distance display to follow the victim's signal. This will often be curved. Analog beacon users will need to adjust your sensitivity control. Move as fast as possible until you reach a distance of about three meters from the victim.

3. Fine Search/Pinpointing
Slow down and pay close attention to your distance readings; directional arrows are less important. Get your beacon as close as possible to the snow surface. Once the lowest distance reading is found, search along the perpendicular axis for an even lower reading. When the lowest reading is confirmed, don't hesitate. Start probing!

(1) Signal Search

<20m> ↑ ↑ <20m>

←40m→ ←40m→

(2) Coarse Search

(3) Fine Search

avalanche path

avalanche path

single searcher search path

multiple searchers search paths

To find an avalanche educator or BCA Beacon Training Park near you, check out www.backcountryaccess.com/education.

  Tracker When ease of use matters most. The most trusted name in snow safety.

BCA

---

find the smallest number. Pull out your probe and probe outward in a spiraling circle from that point. When you hit something, leave the probe in place and get ready to dig.

With Multiple Rescuers

If you have partners, make sure all of you turn your transceivers to Search the minute you determine the scene is safe. Often people forget, which can cause confusion for searchers, so be sure to say, "Turn your transceiver to Search" out loud for everyone to hear. Cellphones and other electronic devices can affect avalanche transceivers, especially in search mode. The safest way to avoid this is to turn your cellphone, MP3 player or GoPro off whenever you are wearing your beacon. At a minimum make sure the electronic device is at least 20 inches from your transceiver at all times.

Now assign tasks. Usually it's most efficient to have just one person do the beacon search if there is only one person caught in the slide. Have this person start searching immediately. In the meantime, another person can pull out his or her probe and begin to look around the avalanche path for any signs—skis, poles, mittens, or hats for example. If a sign is located, probe downhill of it just in case your friend happens to be nearby. Another person can also do a quick transceiver check and probe around spots where the avalanche slowed and debris has piled up, like above a tree or in a depression, just in case your partner is there. While this is taking place, the primary searcher continues following his or her beacon.

After checking obvious spots, the extra searchers can join the primary searcher to help probe and dig.

Any people in your party who do not have a job can pull out their shovels to be ready to dig when you've pinpointed the placement of the victim.

Shoveling

Shoveling out an avalanche victim is not intuitive. You don't just start digging straight down on top of the person. That compresses his already small air pocket and leaves you with a narrow hole that's too small to actually get anyone out through.

Rather start digging downhill of the probe marking the buried person's location. You should start about 1.5 times as far from the probe as your buddy is buried. If you have a bunch of people, you can arrange yourself in a V-shape, small end toward the victim. The shoveler at the apex of the V digs down and forward toward the probe, moving snow back behind him. Those along the sides push that snow away and clear out a wide area so you can extract your patient quickly once he's uncovered. Rotate positions frequently to make sure everyone stays strong. Avalanche debris is heavy and hard, and it's difficult to shovel through, so people will tire quickly. Be aware of the fact that there is a person under the snow; so don't just hack away mindlessly. You could cause further injury with your shovel if you aren't careful.

Once you reach your patient, prioritize locating his head and clearing his airway. Then you'll move into the A, B, C, D, E's of first aid (airway, breathing, circulation, disability, environment). Clear his mouth of snow. Check for a pulse. Start CPR. Provide rescue breathing. Stop bleeding using direct pressure and, if possible, elevation. Treat for shock. Get help.

Final Thoughts on Avalanches

Avalanches kill people every year. They kill experts and beginners. They kill people who make stupid mistakes and those who missed something in their calculation of the hazard. To truly learn how to stay safe in avalanche terrain, we need to listen to and learn from one another's stories. Don't be judgmental. We all make bad calls and people aren't going to be willing to share their experiences if they feel as if they are going to be raked over the coals by others when they do. Hearing about someone else's close call helps us build our knowledge and may enable us to recognize hazards we'd miss if we hadn't heard their story.

Remember, snow is beautiful and fun, as well as mysterious and deadly. Treat it with respect, and you're more likely to live to ski another day.

One ski run—no matter how awesome—is not worth dying for. Make sure you approach each descent with humility and a willingness to turn back if conditions aren't right.

CHAPTER 5

Backcountry Etiquette

The downside to improved alpine-touring gear is that it has opened the doors for the hordes to discover the magic only the hearty few could experience just a few years ago. The backcountry is crowded, especially in popular destinations with easy access. Even steep, technical couloirs—like the Apocalypse Couloir in Grand Teton National Park—that used to be skied by only the most hard-core extreme skiers now see almost daily traffic when conditions are good.

In the early 2000s you could pretty much count on being alone when you left the car to head out to ski. That solitude brought freedom with it. There were no rules or regulations guiding your behavior—just common sense and a lot of learning on the fly. That freedom was part of the backcountry's allure for many. But it's hard to find it these days without imposing on someone else's experience. There are just too many of us out there.

The popularity is understandable. Who doesn't love powder skiing? But it does mean that backcountry travelers have the added challenge of dealing with other people when they venture out of bounds. We don't want to have a lot of rules and regulations dictating our behavior in the backcountry, but we also can't act as if we are alone out there and that our decisions and choices won't affect others.

Parking-Area Courtesy

Start your day remembering that everyone out there is looking for the same sweet thing: untracked powder. So be nice. It's becoming pretty normal to hear stories of parking lot rage, especially in popular destinations where parking is limited and lots fill up early.

If you didn't get out of bed early enough to secure a spot right away, be patient. Look around to see if others are waiting for a spot and form a line. Don't pull in after someone pulls out if there are others who got there before you. Try to park tightly to maximize space. Obey the rules. Skiers rely on the

In popular backcountry ski destinations, you may find parking challenging. Be polite and wait your turn for an open spot.

highway workers who clear the roads and make them safe for driving, so don't be a jerk and park in front of a No Parking sign or create a hazard by letting your vehicle hang out into the line of traffic.

Smile and be nice.

Skin Track Courtesy

"Smile and be nice" carries over to your behavior on the uptrack.

In popular destinations, it's likely you will pass and be passed as you travel up the slope. Be courteous and step out of the track to let others by if you are moving slowly or want to take a break. If you are the passer, gently let the folks in front of you know you are behind by saying hello. If they don't immediately step aside to let you by, ask politely if you can pass.

Take care of the track. Try to slide your ski along its uphill edge so you don't break it down. If you do find yourself blowing out the bottom, consider resetting the track rather than complaining about conditions and floundering your way up it anyway.

Don't boot up the skin track. Skin tracks definitely look like the path of least resistance, but your boots will punch down through the snow and create

If you are moving faster than the party ahead of you on the ascent, politely let them know you are there and ask if you can pass.

holes that destroy the track for those skinning up behind you. If you are hiking rather than skinning, make your own path.

Waste Disposal

If you have a dog along, make sure to clean up after it. It's gross to start up the boot track in some places and see the minefield of dog poop on either side of the path. You can either move the poop well away from the path or bag it and pack it out, which is probably the best way to "leave no trace" in a popular area where thousands of dogs may be pooping every winter.

Likewise, if you need to relieve yourself, step off the path. You don't need to go far to urinate, but leaving yellow snow at every rest stop can be pretty nasty. Just go over to a tree or step aside a few feet before you pee.

If you need to defecate, you'll need to be a bit more proactive. Ideally, you should carry a WAG bag or Rest Stop—two of the many brands of personal poop bags for backpackers, climbers, boaters, and skiers available on the market. These bags allow you to carry out your poop easily and hygienically. If you do not have a bag, move well away from the skin track, preferably into a grove of trees. Punch a hole in the snow with your ski pole. Make it deep enough that it will be easy to cover your feces when you are done. Do your business and cover your poop with snow. You can use a snowball for toilet paper if you don't have anything in your pack. Pine needles also work, in the right direction. If you have TP, be sure to place it in a plastic bag and carry it out. This method of waste disposal should only be relied upon as a last resort in popular areas, however.

To protect the resource and ensure everyone has a pleasant experience, plan ahead so you can carry out your poop. Or better yet, do your business before you leave home.

"Dropping In" Etiquette

There are certain unwritten rules that guide the code of behavior for back-country skiers and snowboarders. Breaking these rules can create enemies, so it's a good idea to follow them.

First off, the skiers who broke trail—even if you passed them at the last minute—get the goods first. They did all the work and deserve the reward. It's rude to use their track and then slip by because you are fresh.

If a slope has the potential to avalanche, ski it one at a time. Do this even if you believe conditions are stable. It's a good habit. It allows you to watch one another in case something happens. And it could save lives if

If a slope has the potential to avalanche, ski it one at a time, which means waiting until it is clear below before you drop in. ALLEN O'BANNON

Keep an eye on your buddy while he skis in case you miscalculated and the slope slides.
JOHN FITZGERALD

you misjudged the snowpack. So let each skier get to a safe spot before you drop in.

If you decide that it's safe for more than one skier to be on a slope at a time, talk about it both with your partners and with any other parties that happen to be in the area ready to ski the same line. You want them to understand and agree with your decision if you plan to follow them out onto a slope before they get off it. This may be the case in a tracked-up bowl or during a dry spell when everyone knows and agrees that the snow is bomber. But remember, it's the exception to the rule. Usually you wait your turn.

Try to conserve the snow. That means don't cut huge traversing lines across an entire bowl, chopping up the powder for those who come behind. Try to keep your turns tight, leaving space for the next person to find a clean line. If you are a big party and there are a lot of other people heading for the same slope, consider going somewhere else. Five people quickly track up a slope, so if your party is that big, you may want to head for a less popular destination. Which leads to another consideration: group size.

There is some safety in numbers. You have people to help in the event of an accident or injury. But too many people are a crowd and affect the wilderness experience of those around you. Three or four are good numbers: You've got one person to stay with someone if they get hurt, while one or two others go for help. Two is OK, but you have no backup if something goes wrong. One is cutting your margin of error to nil. Again, OK if you are careful about your choices but risky if the unexpected were to occur. More than five starts to be a crowd. It can be fun to go out with a gang of friends, but think about your impact on other backcountry users and be courteous. Big groups also make it harder to manage avalanche risk.

Concerns About Others

Besides the social impact of other backcountry users, there are real safety issues to think about with regard to crowds skiing out of bounds. If you cause an avalanche, either intentionally to make a slope safe to ski or unintentionally by triggering the slide with a turn, you may take out parties below. It is part of every backcountry traveler's responsibility to be aware of the potential for danger to come from above and plan his or her route to minimize exposure, but as more and more people get out in avalanche terrain, the potential for overlap becomes more and more real, so think about the path below you.

Backcountry skiers also have an effect on roads. In many places some of the most popular ski descents are slide paths routinely controlled by the highway patrol, like Mount Superior in Little Cottonwood Canyon near Salt Lake City. Remember the control work is being done to keep the road open and drivers, not skiers, safe. Follow directions. If the highway patrol has closed an area to bomb the slopes, do not go there. If you are conducting your own slope-control work, don't drop a slide down onto the road. Backcountry skiers rely on having the roads and parking areas plowed, so we need to be courteous to those who do the work for us.

Some popular ski descents are controlled by the highway patrol to protect drivers, not skiers.

Hitchhiking

In many areas it is common for skiers to end up hitching a ride back to their cars after a ski tour. Again, be courteous. If possible, have one person without his or her skis hitch and bring back the car to collect the rest of your party. Wait your turn if another party is already in line for a ride. Don't assume drivers want your dog in their car. If you have a dog along, hitch without it.

If you are less than half a mile or so from your car, don't bother hitching. You can walk or ski along the side of the road. It can be dangerous in places for cars to stop along the highway to pick up or drop off riders, so just hoof it the 20 minutes or so it will take you to get back to your vehicle.

If you have to hike along the road, stay well out of the line of traffic and walk single file against the flow. If a plow comes, climb up onto the bank or cross to the other side of the road to stay out of the way.

Your best bet for getting a ride is to have one member of your party hitchhike without skis from a place where it's easy for a car to pull over. He or she can get a ride to your car and return for the rest of the group.

If you are close to your car or there isn't a safe place for a driver to pull over, your best bet is to tour or hike along the side of the road well away from traffic.

Be Prepared

Everyone has to start somewhere, so there is no shame in being a beginner when you first venture out backcountry skiing. But the time when you could be excused for making stupid decisions because you didn't know any better is long past. You'd have to have your head in the sand to not know avalanches are a hazard when you venture out of bounds in search of powder. Even if most of your prior knowledge comes from ski movies, it's clear that the skiers in the films are wearing backpacks

There's no shame in being a beginner, but it's not an excuse to ignore the hazards of going out into the backcountry. Get educated before you go.

and taking precautions for their safety. So don't go out into the winter environment without the equipment and knowledge you need to minimize your risk. Your ignorance can be a hazard not only to you but also to those around you.

Final Thoughts on Etiquette

In popular backcountry ski destinations, it's not uncommon for tension to develop between user groups, be it skier-skier, skier-driver, skier–snow machiner, even skier with dog versus skier without. Much of this bad feeling can be avoided if users are polite, think of others, and don't abuse the privilege and freedom of skiing in the backcountry.

Attitude is everything. One snotty comment or obscene gesture creates a lot of bad feeling, so swallow that rude comeback, smile, wave at the driver who doesn't pick you up, and be kind and generous. We can't change the fact that more of us are venturing out every year. We *can* try to make sure that we all have a good experience out there.

CHAPTER 6

Putting It All Together

Now that you've read about gear, clothes, technique, hazards, and avalanches, are you ready to head out? Maybe. Or maybe all this information is just overwhelming you. It can be intimidating to pull everything together and feel confident in your ability to navigate the winter world on your own. So don't do it alone. Most backcountry skiers take their first excursions out of bounds with a more experienced friend or guide.

You can find ski guides in most ski towns these days. Your experience with a guide can vary, depending on your desires. You can just follow along blindly, or you can pump your guide for information. If you want to become competent to travel in the winter on your own, be an involved client. Ask your guide what he or she is thinking about and looking at. Ask him or her why you

Pay attention to your more experienced friends, guides, and teachers. Ask questions and watch the way they evaluate slopes to build your knowledge. Don Sharaf

Choose partners who have a risk tolerance similar to yours. You don't want to be forced to ski in terrain where you are uncomfortable. JOHN FITZGERALD

are skiing a particular slope as opposed to another. Use the answers to these questions to begin building up your own knowledge base.

Be careful with the friends you choose to ski with. Make sure you trust their judgment and that they are open to questions and feedback. You don't want to be out in the wilderness with someone who is defensive or reactive.

Part of decision making includes questioning, especially when evaluating avalanche slopes, so you want to make sure you have open and honest communication in your group.

You also want to make sure your risk tolerance is similar to that of the people with whom you travel. If you are more conservative—or more of a thrill-seeker—than others in your party, you may find yourself frustrated or frightened. Seek like-minded individuals to explore with to ensure you have a good experience.

Try to be open to learning every time you head out to ski in the back-country. Don't assume you have seen everything, because you haven't. Every snowpack is different. Every day is different. What was ego-boosting powder one day may be transformed into breakable crust the next. It just takes a little wind, a change in temperature, or some new snow to clean the slate and create a whole new set of conditions for you to evaluate.

And finally, make sure you have an accurate assessment of yourself. That assessment includes not only your skiing ability but also your knowledge of the winter environment with all its inherent hazards. You may be the best skier in the world, but if you don't know anything about avalanches, you have

Make sure you have an accurate understanding of your limits and stay within them when you head out skiing. Low-angle powder can be amazingly fun and safe. John Fitzgerald

Powder skiing is magical and addictive. Choose wisely so you get many more days to enjoy its allure.

no business leaving the resort or getting onto slopes steeper than 30 degrees in the backcountry. Be humble and conservative as you gain experience.

There's a saying in the outdoors world: "Wimp to wimp again." It can be hard to turn around or back off in the backcountry, especially when your friends on social media are posting pictures of themselves skiing sick powder in a steep couloir. There's pressure to be the raddest, baddest skier out there, and your fame lasts only a day or so before someone else has passed you by, upping the ante for the next radical descent. Don't let yourself get sucked into that mind-set. To live to ski again, you need to turn off those voices. You need to make a decision not only for yourself but also for your friends and family who want you to come home at the end of the day. It's important to recognize that sometimes going home is your best choice, even if you may never be able to prove that. Often nothing happens to justify your decision. The slope doesn't spontaneously slide and the weather miraculously improves as you reach your car, leaving you second-guessing your decision to turn around. Don't second-guess. Wimp to wimp again. It's not worth losing your life over one more ski run.

Backcountry skiing in powder is one of the most magical things you may ever do. But it's not an activity to take too lightly. Be smart and have fun.

About the Author

Molly Absolon is a former NOLS instructor, an environmental educator, and outdoor writer. She is the author of the *Backpacker* Magazine Core Skills books *Campsite Cooking*, *Hiking and Backpacking with Kids*, *Trailside Navigation*, *Trailside First Aid*, and *Outdoor Survival*, as well as *Basic Illustrated Winter Hiking and Camping*. She lives in Victor, Idaho.